San Francisco Houses

teNeues

Editor in chief: Paco Asensio

Project coordination and texts: Ana G. Cañizares

Editorial coordination: Haike Falkenberg

Editorial assistant: Cynthia Reschke

Photographs: Roger Casas

Art director: Mireia Casanovas Soley

Layout: Ignasi Gracia i Blanco

Copy-editing: Francesc Bombí-Vilaseca, Matthew Clarke

German translation: Sven Mettner

French translation: Michel Ficerai

Spanish translation: Almudena Sasiain

Published by teNeues Publishing Group

teNeues Publishing Company
16 West 22nd Street, New York, NY 10010, US
Tel.: 001-212-627-9090, Fax: 001-212-627-9511

teNeues Book Division
Kaistraße 18
40221 Düsseldorf, Germany
Tel.: 0049-(0)211-994597-0, Fax: 0049-(0)211-994597-40

teNeues Publishing UK Ltd.
P.O. Box 402
West Byfleet
KT14 7ZF, Great Britain
Tel.: 0044-1932-403509, Fax: 0044-1932-403514

www.teneues.com

ISBN: 3-8238-4526-8

Editorial project: © 2003 **LOFT** Publications

Via Laietana, 32 4º Of. 92
08003 Barcelona, Spain
Tel.: 0034 932 688 088
Fax: 0034 932 687 073

e-mail: loft@loftpublications.com
www.loftpublications.com

Printed by: Cayfosa-Quebecor. Spain. June 2003

Bibliographic information published by Die Deutsche Bibliothek Die Deutsche Bibliothek lists this publication in the Deutsche Nationalbibliografie; detailed bibliographic data is available in the Internet at http://dnb.ddb.de.

Table of Contents

26
21st Street

36
Laidley House

60
Grandview Residence

68
Clinton Park

92
Ward Residence

98
Kohler Residence

122
Fong/Rodríguez House

130
Bernal Heights Residence

154
Minott Residence

162
Lloyd Loft

188
Potrero Hill

196
Lower Pacific Heights

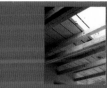
44
Randall Street

52
Windfield Street

76
Eureka Street

84
Small/Shapiro Residence

106
Vonstein Apartment

114
Ghisini/Jacimovic House

138
Magnolia Row

146
Ritch Zoe Studios

172
The Castro

180
Liberty Hill

204
Elsie Street Residence

212
Zircon Place Residence

220 **Kalmbach Residence**

 228 **Grandview House**

 246 **Telegraph Hill Residence**

 254 **Airaghi Residence**

 278 **Martin I**

 288 **Martin III**

 314 **Astrolab House**

 322 **Residence Royale**

 346 **House in Marin County**

 352 **Alvarado Road House**

 368 **Perkins-Herbert Residence**

 376 **Twin Flats**

234

Hammonds Residence

240

Schein Residence

262

Gillipsie/Airaghi Ltd.

270

Corson Residence

296

85 Natoma

304

Oliver Residence

330

Belvedere Residence

338

Cole Valley Residence

360

Barnes/Tenazas Residence

384

Choy/Rowley Residence

392

Shah-Conrad Residence

The Neighborhoods - Die Stadtviertel
Les quartiers - Los barrios

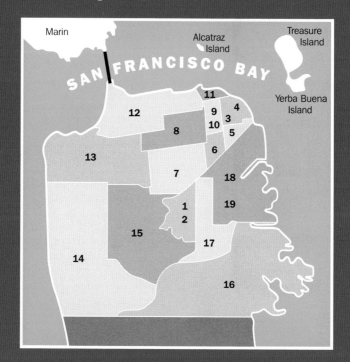

Marin

Alcatraz
Island

Treasure
Island

SAN FRANCISCO BAY

Yerba Buena
Island

11
12
9
10
8
4
3
5
6
13
7
18
1
2
19
15
17
14
16

1. Castro
· Upper end of Market Street, Halloween Parade, Gay Freedom Day Parade
· Oberes Ende der Market Street, Halloween-Parade, Christopher-Street-Day-Parade
· Partie haute de Market Street, parade de Halloween, parade du Gay Freedom Day
· Zona alta de Market Street, desfile de Halloween, desfile del Día del Orgullo Gay

2. Noe Valley
· Pace of its own, restaurants, boutiques and renovated Victorian and Edwardian structures

· Hat einen eigenen Rhythmus, Restaurants, Geschäfte und renovierte viktorianische und eduardianische Gebäude
· Un rythme personnel, restaurants, boutiques et structures victoriennes et edwardiennes rénovées
· Un remanso de paz, restaurantes, tiendas y construciones victorianas y eduardinas remodeladas

3. Chinatown / Northbeach

4. Telegraph Hill
· Stepped streets and gardened lanes topped by Coit Tower

·Steile Straßen und begrünte Wege, über die der Coit Tower ragt
·Rues escarpées et allées paysagères couronnée par la Coit Tower
·Entramado de calles escalonadas y ajardinadas, presididas por la Coit Tower

5. Union Square / Financial District

6. Civic Center
·Central government, cultural events, prominent buildings
·Stadtverwaltung, kulturelle Veranstaltungen, markante Gebäude
·Gouvernement central, événements culturels, immeubles d'importance
·Gobierno Central, eventos culturales, edificios destacados

7. Haight / Western Addition
·Peaceful blend of cultures and lifestyles
·Beschauliche Mischung von Kulturen und Lebensstilen
·Mélange paisible de cultures et de styles de vie
·Mezcla armónica de culturas y estilos de vida diferentes

8. Pacific / Lawel Heights

9. Russian Hill
·Residential, parks, refuge for local writers and artists
·Wohnviertel, Parks, Zufluchtsort für ortsansässige Schriftsteller und Künstler
·Résidences, parcs, havre pour les écrivains et artistes locaux
·Zona residencial, parques, refugio de artistas y escritores locales

10. Nob Hill
·Postcard-perfect scenery, luxurious hotels, finest residences
·Postkartenidylle, Luxushotels, die gediegensten Wohnsitze
·Décor de carte postale, hôtels luxurieux, résidences somptueuses
·Escenografía de postal, hoteles de lujo, elegantes residencias

11. Fisherman's Wharf

12. Marina
·Created in 1915 for the Panama Pacific International Exhibition
·Entstanden 1915 für die Panama Pazifik Internationale Weltausstellung
·Créée en 1915 pour l'Exposition Internationale Panama-Pacifique
·Barrio creado en 1915 para la Exposición Internacional de Panamá y del Pacífico

13. Richmond / 14. Sunset
·Flat, landscaped terrain often coated by a blanket of dense fog
·Flaches landschaftlich gestaltetes Gelände, das oft unter einem dichten Nebelschleier liegt
·Terrain plat et paysager, souvent revêtu d'un dense manteau de brouillard
·Zona llana y ajardinada, cubierta a menudo por una capa de densa niebla

15. Twin Peaks
·Small, quiet town approaching the highest point in the city
·Kleiner, ruhiger Stadtteil nahe der höchsten Erhebung der Stadt
·Petite ville paisible proche du promontoire le plus élevé de la cité
·Pequeña y tranquila localidad, próxima a la parte alta de la ciudad

16. Excelsior / Bayview / Hunters Pt.

17. Mission

18. SOMA (South of Market)
·Area in constant transition, live/work spaces, bars and clubs.
·Gebiet in stetigem Wandel, Räume zum Arbeiten und Wohnen, Bars und Clubs
·Zone en constante transition, espaces séjour/travail, bars et clubs
·Zona en constante evolución, espacios de vivienda y trabajo, bares, clubes

19. Potrero Hill
·Affordable prices, sunny weather and great views
·Erschwingliche Preise, Sonnenschein und herrliche Sicht
·Prix abordables, ensoleillé et vues superbes
·Precios asequibles, zona soleada y dotada de estupendas vistas

San Franciscans love their city. They have even become attached to the fog that has haunted their bay for longer than they can remember. In fact, it is said that when the Coast Guard removed the bay's last foghorn, cries of protest soon brought it back. Only a city with a profound sense of identity and tradition adheres so fervently to its rituals and habits, and San Francisco is one of them. This cultural loyalty makes its presence felt in many aspects of the city today, including its residential architecture. San Franciscans like their city to be known as a hotbed of Victorian architecture, and most want to keep it that way. Against long odds and much resistance, contemporary architecture has made its way slowly but surely into the heart of the beatnik city, giving rise to an influx of rebellious and exciting projects that have upset traditionalists and given the city a reputation for its contribution to the contemporary architectural movement. The defiant and innovative character of this movement is undoubtedly the result of a tumultuous history of cultural movements, social unrest, natural disasters, economic roller coasters and a close relationship with the unique landscape. It is therefore worth taking a quick chronological trip through this city's restless past to discover its idiosyncrasies and better understand the social conditions that have come to influence its architecture and culture.

Funnily enough, the first European visitors to reach the San Francisco Bay Area missed the massive inlet altogether. In 1579 Sir Francis Drake sailed south, straight past the bay, and not long after Spanish explorers seeking refuge from a shipwreck close by also failed to notice the harbor. Nearly 200 years later, Juan Manuel de Ayala became the first European to enter the Golden Gate. A tiny village known as Yerba Buena sprouted up and in 1847 this was renamed San Francisco after Saint Francis of Assisi.

The Gold Rush that began in 1849 lasted a couple of decades before taking a plunge in the late 1870s; nevertheless, the city grew steadily and

Introduction

continued to make its mark as an important financial center. On 18 May 1906, the Big One hit San Francisco. Estimated at 8.3 on the (yet to be invented) Richter Scale, the earthquake did not devastate the city as much as the fires that it caused. A decade of frantic rebuilding and a short-lived revival of the city were followed by the Great Depression, which prompted a number of large-scale public projects that intended to pull the economy out of the slump. Two of the most prominent, the Bay Bridge of 1936 and the Golden Gate Bridge of 1937, remain landmarks of the city today.

The mid-1950s gave rise to the Beat Generation, personified by the up-and-coming poets of San Francisco. Flower Power was born in the 1960s, and at the same time Berkeley revolutionaries were leading worldwide student protests. In the 1970s, San Francisco's gay community took a decisive and loud step out of the closet, and to this day forms an essential part of the city's identity and charm. The second "Big One" in 1989 and the 1991 Oakland firestorm disconcerted San Francisco once again, and in the last decade of the millennium it experienced another period of urban renewal. New neighborhoods, historic buildings and the dot-com boom made San Francisco an increasingly expensive city to live in. But history repeats itself, and at the turn of the millennium the industry plummeted once again, although a swift recovery was soon underway.

Today San Francisco has a population of over 800,000, and is just one of many cities in the Bay Area. The most frequented parts of Frisco include the classy shops around Union Square, the high-rise Financial District, stylish Nob Hill and Russian Hill, Chinatown, North Beach, clubby SoMa (South of Market District) and the gay Castro district. A city built on 43 hills, its steep and curving streets create a unique location that breeds hazardous parking, superhuman bicycle messengers and cable cars registered as the only moving National Historic Landmark in the country. The hilly terrain culminates at the 900-ft high Twin Peaks and Mount Sutro, which provide some of the most breathtaking views of the bay.

All these conditions, produced by the cultural history and physical traits of an evolving metropolis, have influenced the state of its urban residential architecture today. Although the turn of the century did see a significant surge in Modernist architecture, pioneered by the likes of Bernard Maybeck, these works have become old enough to be considered traditional and familiar. San Francisco is a city with 215 historic landmark buildings and 14,000 Victorian homes. The late 1800s left its imprint not only on the city, but also on its people. Steeped in the image of itself as a Victorian city, many of its inhabitants are fiercely set on preserving this character, which makes the city so attractive to both residents and tourists.

Times change, however. The technology boom of the 90s generated younger and wealthier clients keen on unconventional solutions and architects just waiting for the opportunity to provide them. San Francisco's nonconformist spirit rose once again to the surface in the form of shocking new architecture that startled die-hard traditionalists and broke the ice for many young local architects with a desire to create different and modern architecture in their own backyard. Invaluable assistance was provided by several international architects like Daniel Libeskind, Herzog & de Meuron, and Rem Koolhaas, whose works have given the city a breath of fresh air and cleared the way for local architects to make their mark.

This new architecture is often considered unapologetic, shocking and intent on demonstrating that architecture can be good without imitating the past. A careful attention to material and form characterizes this new wave. Traditional Victorian facades have given way to gleaming linear cubes of steel and glass. Stucco and wood are given a make-over and ornamentation has been removed. Double-height spaces, clean lines and unfussy interiors are enhanced by a craftsmanlike use of materials and a pervasive casual approach. Simplicity rules over excess and priority is

given to creating spacious interiors and establishing a close relationship between buildings and landscape. Architects who choose to maintain the Victorian facades and traditional details update the interiors by introducing modern materials and reworked layouts to achieve a unique marriage between past and present.

The most conspicuous effect of this new architecture boom is the proliferation of lofts and home offices in areas like SoMa and the Mission district. Their presence has drastically altered the urban fabric in some parts of the city for the first time in decades. This explosion of innovative, and even radical, architecture in San Francisco is mostly the work of small, young firms whose flexibility and independence allow them to develop big ideas into real projects that larger firms would perhaps shy away from.

The architects and projects featured in this collection represent only a fraction of the body of work produced in San Francisco within the last few years. Small firms as well as bigger, more established names can be appreciated for their innovative and groundbreaking designs. Some are modest, others are striking; but on the whole what they succeed in displaying is a sensitivity to traditional references and an even greater zeal for spawning unconventional designs that often shake up the masses, reminding San Franciscans that their deep-rooted past is just as important as their unfolding future.

Die Einwohner San Franciscos lieben ihre Stadt. Sie hängen sogar an dem Nebel, der ihre Bucht seit ewigen Zeiten heimsucht. Es wird erzählt, dass, als die Küstenwache das letzte Nebelhorn der Bucht entfernte, dieses durch einen Sturm des Protestes schnell zurückgebracht wurde. Nur eine Stadt mit einem tief verwurzelten Identitäts- und Traditionssinn hält vehement an ihren Riten und Gewohnheiten fest wie San Francisco. Diese kulturelle Loyalität ist in vielerlei Hinsicht zu spüren, auch in ihrer Wohnarchitektur. Die Einwohner legen Wert darauf, dass ihre Stadt als Wiege der viktorianischen Architektur bekannt ist, und die meisten möchten dieses Erbe erhalten. Langwierigem Streit und starkem Widerstand zum Trotz fand die zeitgenössische Architektur langsam aber sicher ihren Weg ins Herz der Beatnik-Stadt und führte zu einer Flut rebellischer und hochinteressanter Projekte, welche die Traditionalisten verärgerten und wodurch sich die Stadt zugleich einen Namen für ihren Beitrag zur zeitgenössischen Architekturbewegung machte. Deren herausfordernder und innovativer Charakter ist zweifellos das Ergebnis einer turbulenten Geschichte kultureller Strömungen, sozialer Unruhen, Naturkatastrophen, wirtschaftlicher Umschwünge sowie einer engen Beziehung zu der einzigartigen Landschaft. Es lohnt daher eine kurze Zeitreise durch die ruhelose Vergangenheit dieser Stadt, um ihre Eigenheiten zu entdecken und die gesellschaftlichen Bedingungen besser zu verstehen, die ihre Architektur und Kultur prägen.

Interessant ist, dass die ersten europäischen Besucher, welche die Bay Area erreichten, allesamt die riesige Bucht verpassten. Sir Francis Drake segelte 1579 südlich an der Bucht vorbei, und nicht lange danach verfehlten spanische Entdecker, die ganz in der Nähe Schiffbruch erlitten hatten, auf der Suche nach einem Zufluchtsort den Hafen ebenfalls. Etwa 200 Jahre später war Juan Manuel de Ayala der erste Europäer, der das Golden Gate durchquerte. Es entstand eine winzige Ortschaft namens Yerba Buena, die 1847 nach dem heiligen Franziskus von Assisi in San Francisco umbenannt wurde.

Der 1849 einsetzende Goldrausch dauerte ein paar Jahrzehnte an, bevor er in den späten 1870er Jahren einbrach; dessen ungeachtet wuchs die

Einleitung

Stadt stetig und gewann als wichtiges Finanzzentrum an Bedeutung. Am 18. Mai 1906 wurde San Francisco von einem schweren Erdbeben erschüttert. Das auf eine Stärke von 8,3 auf der (erst noch zu erfindenden) Richterskala geschätzte Beben verwüstete die Stadt weniger als die von ihm verursachten Brände. Einem Jahrzehnt fieberhaften Wiederaufbaus und dem kurzzeitigen erneuten Aufblühen der Stadt folgte die große Depression, die der Auslöser für eine Reihe groß angelegter öffentlicher Vorhaben war, mithilfe derer die schwache Konjunktur angekurbelt werden sollte. Zwei der herausragendsten Projekte – die Bay Bridge von 1936 und die Golden Gate Bridge von 1937 – sind noch heute Wahrzeichen der Stadt.

Die Mitte der 1950er Jahre brachte die Beatgeneration hervor, zu der die vielversprechenden Dichter von San Francisco gehörten. Flower Power kam in den 1960er Jahren auf, während zur selben Zeit die Revolutionäre von Berkeley weltweite Studentenproteste anführten. In den 1970er Jahren „outeten" sich die Homosexuellen San Franciscos entschlossen und lautstark und sind bis heute mit der Identität und dem Charme der Stadt untrennbar verbunden. Das zweite schwere Erdbeben 1989 und die Feuersbrunst von Oakland 1991 erschütterten San Francisco nochmals, und in den folgenden Jahren durchlebte es eine weitere Periode städtischer Erneuerung. Neue Stadtviertel, historische Gebäude und der Boom der New Economy ließen die Preise in der Stadt steigen. Doch die Geschichte verläuft zyklisch, und zur Jahrtausendwende stürzte die Branche in eine Krise, wenngleich sich eine rasche Erholung abzeichnete.

San Francisco hat heute mehr als 800.000 Einwohner und ist nur eine von zahlreichen Städten in der Bay Area. Zu den meist besuchten Orten von Frisco zählen die eleganten Läden rund um Union Square, das hoch in den Himmel ragende Finanzviertel, die stilvollen Nob Hill und Russian Hill, Chinatown, North Beach, das angesagte SoMa (South-of-Market-Viertel) sowie das Schwulenviertel Castro. Die auf 43 Hügeln erbaute Stadt mit ihren steilen und sich windenden Straßen ist ein einzigartiger Ort, der riskante Parklücken, übermenschliche Fahrradkuriere und Cable Cars, die einzigen mobilen Denkmäler des Landes, hervorbringt. Das hügelige Gelände gipfelt in den ca. 275 Meter hohen Twin Peaks und Mount Sutro, von denen aus sich einige der atemberaubendsten Aussichten auf die Bucht bieten.

All diese Bedingungen, Ergebnisse der Kulturgeschichte und physischen Merkmale einer in Entwicklung begriffenen Metropole, haben den Zustand ihrer heutigen städtischen Wohnarchitektur beeinflusst. Obwohl es zur Jahrhundertwende einen bedeutenden Aufschwung der modernen Architektur mit Vorreitern wie Bernard Maybeck gab, sind diese Arbeiten mittlerweile alt genug, um als traditionell und vertraut angesehen zu werden. San Francisco ist eine Stadt mit 215 denkmalgeschützten Gebäuden und 14.000 viktorianischen Häusern. Das ausgehende 19. Jahrhundert prägte nicht nur die Stadt, sondern auch ihre Menschen. Sie ist durchdrungen von dem von sich selbst gemachten Bild einer viktorianischen Stadt, und viele ihrer Einwohner sind sehr darauf bedacht, diesen Charakter zu erhalten, der die Stadt für Einheimische und Touristen zugleich so anziehend macht.

Doch die Zeiten ändern sich. Mit dem Technologieboom der 90er Jahre kamen jüngere und wohlhabendere Kunden mit Lust auf unkonventionellere Lösungen sowie die Architekten, die sich um die Möglichkeit rissen, diese anzubieten. Erneut kam San Franciscos widerspenstiger Geist ans Licht in Form von Anstoß erregender neuer Architektur, welche die eingefleischten Traditionalisten aufschreckte und gleichzeitig das Eis für zahlreiche junge, einheimische Architekten brach, die den Wunsch hatten, eine andere, moderne Architektur in ihrer Stadt zu kreieren. Unschätzbare Hilfe kam von verschiedenen internationalen Architekten wie Daniel Libeskind, Herzog & de Meuron oder Rem Koolhaas, deren Arbeiten frischen Wind in die Stadt brachten und dem Erfolg einheimischer Architekten den Weg ebneten.

Diese neue Architektur wird oftmals als kompromisslos und anstößig angesehen, als Demonstration, die beweisen soll, dass Architektur auch gut sein kann, ohne die Vergangenheit zu imitieren. Charakteristisch für diese neue Bewegung ist ein sorgfältiger Umgang mit Materialien und Formen. Traditionelle viktorianische Fassaden sind schimmernden, geradlinigen

kubischen Formen aus Stahl und Glas gewichen. Stuck und Holz erfuhren einen grundlegenden Wandel, Verzierungen verschwanden. Räume von doppelter Höhe, klare Linien und zwanglose Interieurs kommen durch handwerklichen Umgang mit den Materialien sowie ein durchweg lockeres Herangehen voll zur Geltung. Schlichtheit dominiert das Übermaß, und Vorrang hat die Schaffung großzügiger Räume sowie die enge Beziehung zwischen Gebäuden und Landschaft. Architekten, die den Erhalt der viktorianischen Fassaden und der traditionellen Elemente wählen, aktualisieren das Innere durch moderne Materialien und neue Ausführungen, um Vergangenheit und Gegenwart auf einmalige Art miteinander zu verbinden.

Der auffälligste Effekt dieses neuen Architekturbooms ist die Ausbreitung von Lofts und Wohnbüros in Stadtteilen wie SoMa oder Mission District. Sie haben das Stadtgefüge in einigen Bezirken erstmalig seit Jahrzehnten drastisch verändert. Dieser Ausbruch innovativer oder gar radikaler Architektur ist hauptsächlich das Werk kleiner, junger Firmen, deren Flexibilität und Unabhängigkeit es gestatten, großartige Ideen in wirkliche Projekte umzusetzen, vor denen größere Firmen eventuell zurückschrecken würden.

Die hier aufgenommenen Architekten und Projekte stellen nur einen Bruchteil der in den letzten Jahren ausgeführten Arbeiten dar. Die innovativen und bahnbrechenden Entwürfe kleiner Firmen wie auch größerer, etablierterer Namen können gewürdigt werden. Von bescheiden, bis beeindruckend – im Ganzen verdeutlichen sie die Sensibilität gegenüber der Tradition und eine noch stärkere Begeisterung für unkonventionelle Entwürfe, die oft den zufälligen Passanten irritieren und die Einwohner San Franciscos daran erinnern, dass die vor ihnen liegende Zukunft genauso wichtig ist wie ihre tief verwurzelte Vergangenheit.

Les San Franciscains aiment leur cité. Ils se sont même attachés au brouillard hantant leur baie depuis des temps immémoriaux. En fait, il paraît que lorsque les gardes côte ont retiré la dernière corne de brume, le vent de protestation l'a rapidement imposée de nouveau. Seule une ville avec un sens aussi profond de l'identité et de la tradition que San Francisco peut adhérer avec une telle ferveur à ses us et coutumes. Cette fidélité culturelle se fait sentir dans maints aspects de la vie quotidienne de la cité aujourd'hui, incluant son architecture résidentielle. Les San Franciscains apprécient le fait que leur cité soit reconnue comme un haut lieu de l'architecture victorienne et veulent la préserver ainsi. Contre tout attente et une résistance farouche, l'architecture contemporaine a toutefois creusé son sillon, lentement mais sûrement, au cœur de la ville beatnik, donnant lieu à un influx de projets rebelles et passionnants ayant secoué les traditionalistes et permis à la ville d'apporter sa pierre à l'édifice du mouvement architectural contemporain. Ce mouvement à la personnalité provocatrice et innovante est incontestablement le produit d'une histoire tumultueuse de mouvements culturels, de troubles sociaux, de catastrophes naturelles, d'une vie économique en dent de scie et d'une relation étroite avec un cadre unique. Il est donc intéressant de passer rapidement en revue la chronologie du passé agité de la cité afin d'y découvrir ses idiosyncrasies et mieux comprendre les conditions sociétales ayant influencé son architecture et sa culture.

Étrangement, les premiers visiteurs européens à atteindre la région de San Francisco sont passés complètement à côté de la vaste baie. En 1579, Sir Francis Drake doublait la baie, par le Sud, et peu de temps après, des explorateurs espagnols en quête d'un refuge après une avarie manquaient également le port naturel. Quelque 200 ans plus tard, Juan Manuel de Ayala devenait le premier Européen à passer le Golden Gate. Un petit village du nom de Yerba Buena vit le jour pour être rebaptisé, en 1847, San Francisco en mémoire de Saint François d'Assise.

La ruée vers l'or, débutant en 1849, dura presque trois décennies avant de s'effondrer à la fin des années 1870. Cependant, la cité poursuivait

Introduction

son développement constant et s'imposait comme centre financier d'importance. Le 18 mai 1906, le « Big One » secouait San Francisco. Estimé à 8,3 sur l'échelle (encore en devenir) de Richter, le tremblement de terre dévasta moins la ville en lui même que par les incendies qu'il engendra. Une décennie de reconstruction frénétique et un renouveau éphémère de la cité furent suivis par la Grande dépression, origine de nombre de projets publics à grande échelle destinés à tirer l'économie hors de sa léthargie. Deux constructions éminente, le pont de la baie, en 1936, et le pont du Golden Gate, en 1937, demeurent des sites essentiels de la ville aujourd'hui.

Les années 1950 voyaient la naissance de la génération beat, personnifiée par les poètes d'avenir de San Francisco. Le Flower Power naissait dans les années 1960 et, parallèlement, les révolutionnaires de Berkeley menaient les mouvements de manifestation étudiants dans le monde entier. Dans les années 1970, la communauté gay de San Francisco sortait définitivement et manifestement du placard pour former, actuellement, une partie essentielle de l'identité et du charme de la ville. Le second « Big One », en 1989 et la tempête de feu de 1991 à Oakland secouaient une fois de plus San Francisco. La décennie précédant le nouveau millénaire voyait ainsi une nouvelle période de renouveau urbain. De nouveaux quartiers, des bâtiments historiques et le boom des point.com faisaient de San Francisco une ville de plus en plus hors de prix pour ses résidents. Mais, l'histoire se répétant, au passage du millénaire l'économie plongeait de nouveau dans le marasme... bien qu'une reprise soit déjà dans l'air.

San Francisco compte aujourd'hui plus de 800 000 habitants et est l'une des villes de la région de la baie. Les hauts lieux du tourisme de Frisco incluent les boutiques de luxe près d'Union Square, le florissant quartier financier, le chic de Nob Hill et de Russian Hill, Chinatown, North Beach, le nocturne SoMa (South of Market District) et le quartier gay de Castro. Une ville construite sur 43 collines, ses rues pentues et courbes créant un emplacement unique engendrant un stationnement digne de la haute voltige, des messagers cyclistes surhumains et des tramways reconnus comme les seuls Monuments historiques nationaux mobiles du pays. Le terrain vallonné culmine à 275 m, à Twin Peaks et Mount Sutro, offrant là quelques uns des panoramas les plus éblouissants de la baie.

Toutes ces conditions, produits de l'histoire culturelle et des traits physiques d'une métropole en pleine évolution, ont influencé l'état de son architecture résidentielle urbaine présente. Bien que le tournant du siècle ait vu une poussée significative de l'architecture moderniste, comptant Bernard Maybeck parmi ses pionniers, ces travaux sont désormais suffisamment chargés d'histoire pour être devenus traditionnels et familiers. San Francisco est une ville affichant 215 monuments historiques nationaux et 14 000 résidences victoriennes. La fin du 19ème siècle a laissé son empreinte non seulement sur la ville mais aussi sur ses habitants. Pénétrés de l'image de la cité victorienne, ses habitants sont farouchement décidés à préserver cette personnalité, ce qui rend la ville si attirante tant pour les résidents que pour les touristes.

Mais les temps changent. Le boom technologique des années 90 a vu l'apparition de clients plus jeunes et plus riches, affamés de solutions peu conventionnelles et d'architectes saisissant la balle au bond et répondant à leurs attentes. L'esprit non conformiste de San Francisco s'est réveillé pour apparaître sous la forme d'une nouvelle architecture choquante, surprenant les traditionalistes à tout crin et ouvrant la voie à nombre de jeunes architectes locaux, désireux de créer une architecture moderne et différente pour leur propre compte. Plusieurs architectes internationaux ont prêté une assistance inestimable, ainsi Daniel Libeskind, Herzog & de Meuron et Rem Koolhaas. Leurs travaux ont offert à la ville une bouffée d'air frais et tracé la piste pour que les architectes locaux puissent s'imposer.

Cette nouvelle architecture est souvent considérée comme non repentante, choquante et une tentative pour démontrer que l'architecture peut être bonne sans avoir à imiter le passé. Une attention particulière au matériaux et aux formes caractérise cette nouvelle vague. Les façades

victoriennes traditionnelles ont laissé place à des cubes linéaires miroitants d'acier et de verre. Stuc et bois prennent un coup de jeune et les ornementations disparaissent. Les espaces à double hauteur, les lignes claires et les intérieurs sobres sont mis en valeur par un réel savoir faire dans l'usage des matériaux et une approche détendue très convaincante. La simplicité l'emporte sur l'excès et la priorité est donnée à la création d'intérieurs spacieux et d'une relation étroite entre les constructions et le paysage. Les architectes optant pour la préservation des façades victoriennes et les détails traditionnels rénovent les intérieurs en introduisant des matériaux modernes et en refaçonnant les dispositions afin de célébrer un mariage unique entre le passé et le présent.

L'effet le plus manifeste de ce nouveau boom architectural porte sur la prolifération des lofts et des espaces de vie/travail dans des zones comme SoMa et Mission district. Leur présence a théâtralement altéré le tissu urbain en certains endroits de la ville, pour la première fois depuis des décennies. Cette explosion d'architecture innovante, voire radicale, à San Francisco est essentiellement l'œuvre de cabinets petits et nouveaux dont la flexibilité et l'indépendance leur permettent de développer de grandes idées en des projets réels, à même d'effrayer des firmes plus importantes.

Les architectes et projets présentés dans cet ouvrage représentent une fraction seulement de l'immense travail effectué à San Francisco ces dernières années. De petits cabinets d'architecture comme des entreprises plus connues peuvent être appréciés pour leurs concepts innovants et révolutionnaires. Certains sont modestes, d'autres surprenants, mais, dans l'ensemble, ils affichent une sensibilité aux références traditionnelles et un zèle encore plus conséquent pour diffuser des designs peu conventionnels troublant le passant et rappelant aux San Franciscains que leur passé aux traditions immémoriales est aussi important que leur futur sans cesse renouvelé.

Los habitantes de San Francisco aman su ciudad. Están ineludiblemente unidos a la bruma que mora su bahía desde tiempos inmemoriales. De hecho se dice que cuando la guardia costera dejó de utilizar la última sirena de la niebla, hubo tantas protestas que tuvo que reutilizarla. Sólo una ciudad con un profundo sentido de la identidad y de la tradición se aferra tan fervientemente a sus rituales y hábitos, y San Francisco es una de ellas. Esta lealtad cultural hace su presencia en muchos aspectos de la ciudad actual, incluyendo la arquitectura residencial. A los habitantes de San Francisco les gusta que su ciudad sea conocida como un emblema de la arquitectura victoriana, y la mayoría quiere que eso siga siendo así. Pero contra viento y marea, la arquitectura contemporánea ha seguido un camino lento pero seguro hasta alcanzar el corazón de la ciudad beatnik, dando origen a un flujo de proyectos rebeldes y apasionantes que, por un lado, han escandalizado a los tradicionalistas y, por otro, han dado a la ciudad una reputación por su contribución a las formas de construcción contemporáneas. El carácter desafiante e innovador de este movimiento es, sin duda, el resultado de una tumultuosa historia de corrientes culturales, desórdenes sociales, desastres naturales, altibajos económicos y una estrecha relación con un paisaje singular. Por ello merece la pena dar un pequeño paseo cronológico por el pasado agitado de la ciudad para descubrir su idiosincrasia y entender mejor las condiciones sociales que han influido en su arquitectura y en su cultura, en general.

Curiosamente, los primeros europeos que alcanzaron el área de la bahía de San Francisco pasaron por alto la gran ensenada en su conjunto. En 1579, Sir Francis Drake navegando hacia el sur, pasó de largo por la zona, y no mucho después, unos exploradores españoles buscaron refugio en un naufragio muy cerca de allí, pero sin llegar hasta ella. Casi doscientos años más tarde, Juan Manuel de Ayala fue el primer europeo en entrar en el Golden Gate. Allí surgió una pequeña villa conocida como Yerba Buena que en 1847 fue rebautizada como San Francisco en honor al santo de Asís.

La fiebre del oro, que comenzó en 1849, duró un par de décadas hasta desvanecerse a finales de los años de 1870; sin embargo, la ciudad siguió

Introducción

creciendo y se convirtió en un importante centro comercial. El 18 de mayo de 1906, el gran terremoto sacudió San Francisco. Con una intensidad estimada de 8,3 en la escala de Richter (que aún no existía) el movimiento sísmico no devastó la ciudad tanto como los incendios que se desataron. A una década de reconstrucción frenética y una corta reanimación de la ciudad, le siguió la Gran Depresión, que provocó la realización de varios proyectos públicos de gran escala en un intento de reanimar la economía. Dos de los más importantes, el Bay Bridge de 1936 y el Golden Gate Bridge de 1937, se han convertido en emblemas de la ciudad.

A mediados de la década de 1950 surgió la Beat Generation, personificada por los prometedores poetas de San Francisco. El Flower Power nació en la década de 1960, al tiempo que los revolucionarios de Berkeley lideraban las protestas estudiantiles internacionales. En los años en torno a 1970, la comunidad gay de San Francisco dio un decisivo paso al «salir del armario», y desde ese día forma una parte esencial de la identidad y del encanto de la ciudad. El segundo terremoto de 1989 y el incendio de Oakland de 1991 castigaron una vez más a San Francisco, que en la última década del milenio experimentó otro período de renovación urbana. Nuevos barrios, edificios históricos y el auge de las empresas punto com hicieron de San Francisco una ciudad cada vez más cara para vivir. Pero la historia se repite, y con el nuevo milenio la industria cayó de nuevo en una gran crisis, aunque enseguida se vieron indicios de una rápida recuperación.

Hoy en día, San Francisco tiene una población de más de 800.000 habitantes, y es una de las varias ciudades sitas en torno a la bahía. Las partes más frecuentadas de Frisco incluyen las exclusivas tiendas de la zona de Union Square, el próspero Distrito Financiero, las elegantes Nob Hill y Russian Hill, Chinatown, North Beach, el noctámbulo SoMa (South of Market District) y el distrito gay de Castro. Las calles empinadas y sinuosas de esta ciudad construida sobre 43 colinas, hacen de ella una localización única en la que el aparcamiento es una aventura y los mensajeros en bicicletas, seres sobrehumanos. Estas calles están recorridas por un tranvía que es el único patrimonio móvil de todo el país declarado de interés histórico nacional. El terreno lleno de colinas culmina en el Twin Peaks y Mount Sutro, de 270 metros de altura, que ofrecen una de las más impresionantes vistas sobre la bahía.

Todas esas características, derivadas de la historia cultural y los rasgos orográficos de una metrópoli en expansión, han influido en el estado de la arquitectura residencial urbana actual. Aunque a principios del siglo XX, la arquitectura moderna tuvo un auge significativo, liderada por pioneros como Bernard Maybeck, esos trabajos tienen hoy la suficiente solera como para ser considerados tradicionales y familiares. San Francisco es una ciudad con 215 edificios históricos protegidos y 14.000 casas victorianas. Así los últimos años del siglo XIX dejaron una impronta no sólo en la ciudad, sino en sus gentes. Anclados en la imagen de ciudad victoriana, muchos habitantes luchan firmemente para preservar su carácter, que hace la ciudad tan atractiva para residentes y turistas.

Sin embargo, los tiempos cambian. El auge tecnológico de la década de 1990 hizo surgir una generación de clientes jóvenes y pudientes que gustaban de soluciones poco convencionales, y de arquitectos deseosos de aprovechar la oportunidad que se les brindaba. El espíritu inconformista de San Francisco emergía una vez más en forma de una arquitectura nueva y chocante que sobresaltaba a los más tradicionalistas y rompía el hielo para muchos jóvenes arquitectos locales con deseos de crear proyectos de construcción diferentes y modernos en su propia ciudad. En su propósito recibieron la ayuda inestimable de varios arquitectos de renombre internacional como Daniel Libeskind, Herzog & de Meuron, y Rem Koolhaas, cuyos trabajos dieron a la ciudad un soplo de aire fresco y abrieron el camino a los arquitectos locales para que crearan su propio estilo.

Este nuevo movimiento, considerado como libre de complejos y rompedor, intenta demostrar que la arquitectura puede ser buena sin imitar el pasado. Una cuidadosa atención a los materiales y formas caracteriza esta nueva ola. Las tradicionales fachadas vitorianas han dejado vía libre

a brillantes cubos lineales de acero y cristal; el estuco y la madera ya no se utilizan de la manera convencional y la ornamentación no resulta imprescindible. Espacios de doble altura, líneas claras e interiores sencillos cobran realce por un uso casi artesano de materiales y la omnipresencia de lo informal. Las reglas de la sencillez tienen ahora prioridad ante el exceso, para crear espacios interiores y establecer una estrecha relación entre edificios y entorno. Por otro lado, los arquitectos que eligen mantener las fachadas victorianas y los detalles tradicionales actualizan los interiores introduciendo materiales modernos y trazados remodelados para lograr un maridaje único entre presente y pasado.

El efecto más remarcable de este nuevo boom arquitectónico es la proliferación de lofts y casas estudio en áreas como SoMa y el distrito de Mission. Su presencia ha alterado drásticamente la fábrica urbana en algunas zonas de la ciudad por primera vez en décadas. Esta explosión de arquitectura innovadora e incluso radical de San Francisco se debe, sobre todo, al trabajo de pequeños y jóvenes estudios de arquitectura cuya flexibilidad e independencia permiten convertir grandes ideas en proyectos reales que muchas empresas importantes rechazarían.

Los arquitectos y proyectos reflejados en esta colección representan sólo una fracción del trabajo desarrollado en San Francisco en los últimos años. Aquí se puede apreciar los diseños innovadores y rompedores tanto de pequeñas empresas como de firmas más establecidas. Algunos son discretos, otros impresionantes. Pero todos ellos tienen en común una gran sensibilidad hacia las referencias tradicionales y un gran entusiasmo por engendrar diseños poco convencionales que suelen confundir a la opinión pública, recordando a los habitantes de San Francisco que el futuro que se abre ante ellos es tan importante como su profundamente enraizado pasado.

21st Street

ANNE FOUGERON
viv@fougeron.com

The remodeling of this Victorian home explores the effects of transparency in the literal and figurative sense. Exterior and interior glass walls create continuous, multiple readings of space, depending on the time of day. The glass box containing the bathroom is the perfect buffer between the communal nature of the kitchen and the intimacy of the bathroom. During the day, light passes through the south-facing kitchen and into the bathroom, creating a bright, warm atmosphere. In contrast, the translucent volume glows green at night with the help of fluorescent gels. The architects integrated the existing Victorian elements and reinterpreted them by adding customized steel details.

Der Umbau dieses viktorianischen Hauses spürt den Effekten der Transparenz nach – im wörtlichen wie im übertragenen Sinne. Außen- und Innenwände aus Glas bieten je nach Tageszeit fortlaufende und vielfältige Rauminterpretationen. Die Glasumfassung des Badezimmers bildet die perfekte Schutzschicht zwischen dem offenen Charakter der Küche und der Intimität des Bades. Tagsüber dringt Licht durch die Küche ins Bad und sorgt für eine helle, freundliche Atmosphäre. Nachts hingegen schimmert der Glaskörper aufgrund fluoreszierender Gele grün. Die Architekten integrierten die vorhandenen viktorianischen Elemente und gaben ihnen eine neue Interpretation im Zusammenspiel mit maßgefertigten Details aus Stahl.

Completion date: **2002**

La rénovation de cette maison victorienne explore les effets de la transparence, au propre et au figuré. Des parois vitrées intérieures et extérieures créent des lectures multiples et continues de l'espace, selon l'heure. La pièce en verre contenant le bain offre une protection parfaite entre la nature commune de la cuisine et l'aspect privé de la salle de bains. De jour, la lumière entre par la cuisine exposée au Sud et dans le bain, créant une atmosphère chaude et lumineuse. Par contraste, le volume translucide devient vert la nuit grâce à des gels fluorescents. Les architectes ont intégré les éléments victoriens existants pour les réinterpréter à l'aide de détails métalliques.

La remodelación de esta vivienda victoriana explora los efectos de la transparencia en sentido literal y figurativo. Paredes exteriores e interiores de cristal crean múltiples lecturas del espacio dependiendo de la hora del día. La caja acristalada que acoge el baño es la protección perfecta entre la privacidad inherente a este espacio y la naturaleza comunal de la cocina. Así se logra además que durante el día la luz llegue al cuarto de aseo a través de la cocina orientada hacia el sur, creando una atmósfera brillante y cálida. Por la noche, el volumen traslúcido resplandece en verde con la ayuda de geles fluorescentes. El arquitecto supo integrar los elementos victorianos y reinterpretarlos con el uso de detalles en acero.

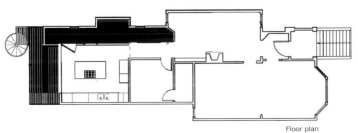

Floor plan

Laidley House

ANNE FOUGERON
viv@fougeron.com

The intention behind this San Francisco conversion was to unify the existing facade while creating several ways of guiding light into the interior spaces. The intervention focused on the front five feet of the structure. The one-dimensional nature of the house was transformed into a dialogue of transparent and solid layers with strips of glazing in-between. A skylight integrated into the new exterior concrete structure gives light onto the dining area inside. The protruding window stretching vertically up the facade defines the double-height void inside the house. The lower level consists of the living area, while the mezzanine overlooking it contains the bedroom.

Der Umbau dieses Hauses in San Francisco sollte die vorhandene Fassade vereinheitlichen sowie auf verschiedene Weise Licht in die Innenräume leiten. Im Mittelpunkt standen die vorderen 1,5 m des Tragwerks. Die eindimensionale Natur des Hauses wurde in einen Dialog transparenter und massiver Schichten mit dazwischen liegenden verglasten Bereichen verwandelt. Ein in das neue äußere Betonskelett integriertes Dachfenster erhellt den Essbereich. Das vortretende, vertikal über die Fassade laufende Fenster prägt den Raum von doppelter Höhe im Inneren des Hauses. Im unteren Stockwerk befindet sich der Wohnbereich, im sich darauf öffnenden Zwischenschengeschoss das Schlafzimmer.

Completion date: **2000**

L'intention derrière cette réforme était d'unifier la façade existante tout en implémentant plusieurs techniques guidant la lumière vers l'intérieur. L'intervention s'est centrée sur le 1,5 m de l'avant de la structure. La nature unidimensionnelle de la maison a été transformée en un dialogue de couches solides et transparentes intercalées de bandes vitrées. Une claire-voie intégrée à la nouvelle structure extérieure donne sur le coin repas intérieur. La fenêtre en saillie parcourant verticalement la façade définit la double hauteur de vide dans la demeure. Le niveau inférieur comprend un séjour et la mezzanine le surplombant abrite une chambre.

La intención de esta reforma fue unificar la fachada preexistente implementando diferentes medios para conseguir que la luz entrase en los espacios interiores. La intervención se centró en la fachada a 1,5 m de la estructura. La naturaleza unidimensional de la casa se transformó en un diálogo de trazados transparentes y sólidos con cristaleras incorporadas. Una claraboya construida en la nueva estructura exterior de hormigón abre el área del comedor. La ventana saliente que corre verticalmente a lo largo de la fachada define el hueco de doble altura dentro de la vivienda. El nivel inferior acoge un salón y un entrepiso orientado hacia el interior en el que se encuentra el dormitorio.

Randall
Street

LEVY ART & ARCHITECTURE
karen@10d.com

The design for this Noe Valley home was based on the premise of creation by removal. The house was reoriented to face the rear garden and the formal parlors along the street were converted into entrance and circulation spaces with access to the new bedrooms below. The bedroom and utility porch that previously existed at the back of the house were removed to make way for a living space looking east to the skyline. Inside, a bright combination of white and green enlivens the living areas, which are characterized by the network of wooden beams across the ceiling. A blue wall acts as a backdrop for the striking white bed in the master bedroom.

Der Entwurf dieses Hauses in Noe Valley basiert auf der Prämisse von Neugestaltung durch Rückbau. Das Haus wurde zum Garten an der Rückseite hin neu ausgerichtet und die Wohnräume zur Straße wurden in Eingangs- und Zugangsbereiche verwandelt, die nach unten zu den neuen Schlafzimmern führen. Der ehemalige Vorbau zum Schlafen und Wirtschaften an der Rückseite des Hauses wich einem Wohnraum mit Blick nach Osten auf die Skyline. Eine Kombination frischer Weiß- und Grüntöne belebt die Wohnbereiche, deren Charakter von der Holzbalkenkonstruktion an der Decke geprägt wird. Im großen Schlafzimmer bildet eine blaue Wand die Kulisse für ein Bett in blendendem Weiß.

Completion date: **1997**

Le design de cette demeure de Noe Valley repose sur l'idée de la suppression créative. La maison a été réorientée face à l'arrière-jardin et les petits salons sur rue convertis en entrées et espaces de circulation, accédant aux nouvelles chambres, juste en dessous. La chambre et le porche, auparavant à l'arrière de la maison, ont été supprimés pour offrir un espace de vie regardant l'horizon, à l'est. À l'intérieur, une palette de blanc et de vert anime les aires de séjour, caractérisées par la charpente en bois parcourant le plafond. Un mur bleu sert de toile de fond au lit blanc immaculé de la chambre principale.

El diseño de esta casa de Noe Valley se basó en las premisas de la creación por eliminación. La vivienda se reorientó hacia el jardín trasero, y las estancias que daban a la calle se transformaron en espacios de circulación y entrada para acceder a los nuevos dormitorios del piso inferior. La alcoba y el porche recocina traseros se eliminaron en favor de un salón con vistas al este. En el interior, una fresca paleta de tonos blancos y verdes da vida a las áreas de estar, demarcadas por un armazón de vigas de madera que cruzan el techo. Una pared azul hace las veces de telón de fondo de la blanquísima cama del dormitorio principal.

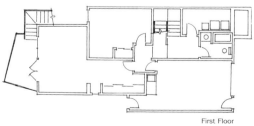

First Floor

Second Floor

Windfield Street

LEVY ART & ARCHITECTURE
karen@10d.com

The aim of this renovation was to create a loft-like interior in a two-story Edwardian home in Bernal Heights. Architects replaced the conventional narrow, enclosed staircase with a sweeping sculptural steel stairwell that conveys movement and elegance. The entire space upstairs was opened up by removing interior walls and creating openings in the ceiling. A triangular transom window that follows the line of the gable roof was installed just above the sliding doors. The interiors are clean-cut and straightforward, with neutral colors and broad spaces left to absorb the abundant daylight. A few wooden beams and a ventilation duct serve as both functional and aesthetic components of the space.

Ziel der Renovierung war es, ein loft-ähnliches Interieur in einem zweige-schossigen eduardianischen Haus in Bernal Heights zu schaffen. Die Archi-tekten ersetzten die konventionelle enge Treppe durch eine schwungvolle Stahltreppenskulptur, die Bewegung und Eleganz vermittelt. Das Oberge-schoss wurde durch das Entfernen von Wänden und den Einbau von Dachfens-tern erweitert. Ein dem Satteldach fol-gendes dreieckiges Sprossenfenster wurde direkt über den Schiebetüren eingebaut. Das Interieur ist geradlinig und schlicht, die neutralen Farben und großzügigen freien Räume nehmen reichlich Tageslicht auf. Holzbalken und ein Entlüftungsrohr gehören zu den ebenso funktionalen wie ästhetischen Komponenten des Raums.

Completion date: **2000**

Cette rénovation voulait créer l'intérieur d'un loft dans une maison edwardienne de deux niveaux à Bernal Heights. Les architectes ont remplacé l'escalier étroit et fermé conventionnel par une volée métallique sculpturale offrant mouvement et élégance. Au-dessus, l'espace est grand ouvert grâce à la suppression des murs intérieurs et l'ajout d'ouvertures au plafond. Une fenêtre de traverse triangulaire, suivant la ligne du toit à pignons, s'invite au-dessus des portes coulissantes. Les tons neutres et les vastes espaces des intérieurs, simples et soignés, absorbent l'abondante lumière du jour. Quelques poutres en bois et un tuyau d'aération forment les éléments fonctionnels et esthétiques de l'espace.

El objetivo de la reforma fue crear un loft en una casa eduardina de dos pisos de Bernal Heights. Los arquitectos sustituyeron la estrechez convencional y envolvieron la escalera con una amplia y escultural caja de acero que aporta movimiento y elegancia. El espacio del piso superior se abrió totalmente con la eliminación de los tabiques y la creación de aberturas en el techo. Asimismo, sobre las puertas corredizas se instaló una ventana de dintel triangular que sigue la línea del tejado a dos aguas. El interior es claro y sencillo con colores neutrales y espacios amplios que absorben la abundante luz diurna. Unas pocas vigas de madera y un conducto de ventilación son elementos especiales funcionales y estéticos a la vez.

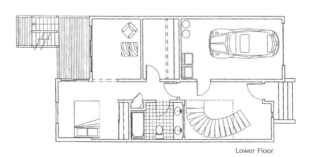

Lower Floor

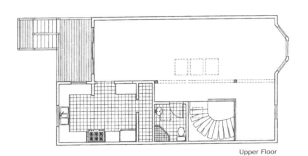

Upper Floor

Grandview Residence

LEVY ART & ARCHITECTURE
karen@10d.com

This residence, with a sculptural, highly worked mass running along the building's main facade, was determined by the architects' response to its location between a boxy building some fifty years old and a recently completed contemporary home. The forms of the neighboring building were subtly incorporated, while adapting to the typical front-porch layout. The project involved the addition of a new bedroom, bathroom, lounge, deck and rooftop garden to an existing garage structure. The bedroom was placed adjacent to the new living area in the form of an open suite, while folding doors provide the option of converting the bedroom into a dark cocoon for sleeping.

Mit diesem Wohnhaus mit einer skulptural bearbeiteten Hauptfassade antwortet der Architekt auf den Baubestand zu beiden Seiten: ein aus der Mitte des 19. Jahrhunderts stammendes kastiges Gebäude und ein zeitgenössischer Neubau. Die Formen der Nachbargebäude wurden subtil aufgegriffen, indem sie in die typische Anlage des straßenseitigen Vorbaus eingepasst wurden. Das Projekt beinhaltete den Anbau eines neuen Schlaf- und Badezimmers, eines Aufenthaltsbereichs, einer Dachterrasse und eines Dachgartens an eine existierende Garage. Das Schlafzimmer liegt als offene Suite neben dem neuen Wohnbereich, wobei mithilfe von Falttüren die Möglichkeit besteht, es in eine dunkle Schlafkammer zu verwandeln.

Completion date: **2000**

Entre un édifice du milieu du 19ième siècle et une maison contemporaine récente, cette résidence présente la réponse de l'architecte à son contexte, consistant en une masse sculpturale manipulée le long de la façade principale du bâtiment. Les formes des maisons voisines ont été incorporées subtilement en adaptant la disposition typique du porche. Le projet a impliqué l'ajout de chambres, bain, coin repos, terrasse et jardin sur le toit à la structure en garage existante. La chambre a été placée à côté du nouveau séjour sous la forme d'une suite ouverte et les portes pliantes permettent de convertir la chambre en un coin sombre pour dormir.

Situada entre un edificio de formas cúbicas de mediados del siglo XIX y una casa totalmente contemporánea, esta residencia es la respuesta del arquitecto al contexto, que consiste en una masa escultural manipulada a lo largo de la fachada principal de la construcción. Las formas del edificio vecino se incorporaron sutilmente para adaptarse al típico trazado de porche delantero. El proyecto incorporó un nuevo dormitorio, un baño, un salón, una cubierta y una azotea ajardinada a la estructura de garaje preexistente. El dormitorio es una suite abierta adyacente a la nueva sala, con puertas plegables que ofrecen la opción de convertirlo en una oscura alcoba.

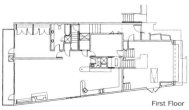

First Floor

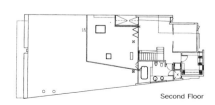

Second Floor

Clinton Park

LEVY ART & ARCHITECTURE
karen@10d.com

A complete renovation added charm to this modest midtown apartment and improved the flow of space and light. The new alignment of the living spaces links one with the other in a series that runs from the front to the back of the building. The bedroom and bathroom were reconfigured and enlarged, and the bedroom was given direct access to the courtyard. The kitchen includes a small eating area in one corner that also opens out onto the garden. A handmade mosaic endows the kitchen area with a personal touch, much like the colorfully patterned tiles that bring the bathroom to life. Overall, the design favors modest materials and crafted detail to obtain simple yet original interiors.

Ein grundlegender Umbau brachte neuen Charme und verbesserte den Raum- und Lichtfluss in dieser einfachen Wohnung inmitten der Stadt. Die Neuordnung verbindet die Wohnbereiche von vorn nach hinten. Schlaf- und Badezimmer wurden umgestaltet und vergrößert, wobei ein direkter Zugang vom Schlafzimmer zum Garten geschaffen wurde. In einer Ecke der Küche wurde ein kleiner Essbereich integriert, ebenfalls zum Garten hin geöffnet. Ein handgefertigtes Mosaik verleiht der Küche einen persönlichen Akzent, ebenso wie das Leben ins Badezimmer bringende, farbenfrohe Fliesenmuster. Das Design favorisiert ingesamt schlichte Materialien und handwerkliche Details und schafft so ein einfaches und zugleich originelles Interieur.

Completion date: **1999**

Une rénovation complète a ajouté du charme et amélioré le flux d'espace et de lumière dans cet appartement du centre. Le nouvel alignement des espaces de vie les relie en une série allant de l'avant à l'arrière. La chambre et le bain ont été reconfigurés et agrandis et la chambre a reçu un accès direct à la cour. La cuisine inclut un petit coin repas dans l'angle du fond, s'ouvrant également sur le jardin. Un dosseret couverts à la main de mosaïques a créé une ambiance personnalisée pour la cuisine, comme les carreaux colorés régénérant le bain. Le design favorise surtout les matériaux modestes et les détails artisanaux pour offrir un intérieur simple mais original.

Una completa reforma dio encanto, una mayor fluidez espacial y más luz a este discreto piso del centro. La nueva alineación comunica entre sí los diferentes espacios de vivienda que se suceden en fila desde la parte frontal a la parte de atrás de la casa. El dormitorio y el baño se reorganizaron y agrandaron. La alcoba tiene ahora acceso directo al patio. La cocina integra en una esquina un pequeño comedor que la abre al jardín. El salpicadero del fregadero de mosaico hecho a mano da un toque personal a la cocina, y las grecas coloridas de los azulejos avivan el baño. El diseño prefiere materiales modestos y detalles artesanales para recrear interiores simples pero originales.

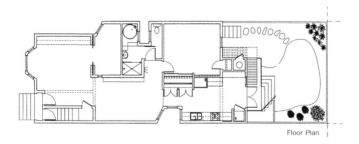

Floor Plan

Eureka Street

PHIL MATHEWS
mathewsarchitect@yahoo.com

Located in the Noe Valley neighborhood, this house is an entirely modern construction of steel, glass and concrete that explores its three-story vertical proportions. The architect qualifies it as "unapologetic", and feels that many new residential structures in this city are "too sentimental and apologetic in trying to imitate old Victorian details and forms". On a corner of a hilltop, the strong cubic form has a modernist look with its recessed glass and steel decks. The rooftop terrace is defined by a steel trellis and the interior is characterized by open space and light, with concrete counters, maple floors, neutral colors and multifunctional rooms to make the most of the floor space.

Dieses im Noe-Valley-Viertel gelegene Haus ist ein gänzlich moderner Bau aus Stahl, Glas und Beton, der sich über drei Etagen in vertikaler Symmetrie erstreckt. Der Architekt bezeichnet es als „kompromisslos" und meint, viele Wohnungsneubauten der Stadt seien „zu sentimental und traditionell, weil sie alte viktorianische Elemente und Formen zu imitieren versuchen". Am Rande einer Hügelkuppe gelegen, wirkt der komplexe Kubus mit seinen zurückgesetzten Decks aus Glas und Stahl modern. Die Dachterrasse wird durch ein Stahlgitter markiert, im Inneren dominieren Raum und Licht, Arbeitsflächen aus Beton, Ahornböden, neutrale Farben und vielfältig nutzbare Räume zur bestmöglichen Nutzung der Grundfläche.

Completion date: **2001**

Voisine de Noe Valley, cette construction entièrement moderne en acier, verre et béton interprète une proportion verticale sur trois étages. L'architecte la veut « non repentante », estimant les nouvelles structures résidentielles de la ville « trop sentimentales et contrites et imitant détails et formes de l'art victorien ». Au sommet d'une colline, le cube solide affiche son modernisme grâce aux vitres encastrées et aux passerelles métalliques. Le toit en terrasse est défini par un treillis de métal et l'intérieur caractérisé par l'espace ouvert et la lumière, les comptoirs de bétons, les parquets d'érable, les tons neutres et les pièces polyvalentes économes en espace au sol.

Esta casa del barrio de Noe Valley es una nueva y moderna construcción de acero, cristal y hormigón vertical de tres pisos. El arquitecto la califica de "sin complejos" y afirma que muchos edificios de la ciudad son "demasiado sentimentales y parecen querer disculparse imitando en demasía las formas y detalles victorianos tradicionales". En lo alto de una colina, la estructura estrictamente cubista presenta un carácter moderno gracias a los nichos de cristal y acero que hay en el piso superior. La azotea está definida por un enrejado de acero.
El interior es un espacio abierto y luminoso con mostradores de hormigón, suelos de arce, colores neutrales y habitaciones multifuncionales para economizar superficie.

First Floor

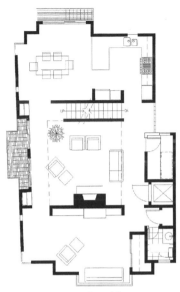

Second Floor

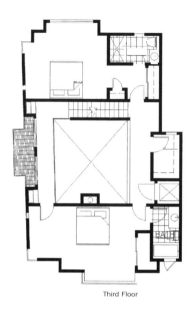

Third Floor

Small/Shapiro Residence

LINDY SMALL
lsmallarch@aol.com

Movement and vision characterize this spatial composition, which comprises a third-level addition to a two-story stick house in the outskirts of San Francisco. The new level consists of a single space shared by a library and a lounge/dining room/kitchen, while the other two levels contain the master bedroom and the children's bedrooms. The new circulation system was dictated by a 50-foot concrete wall that aligns the service areas. The rooms are defined by the materials used on the floor, the height of the ceilings, the thickness of the walls and the structural columns. Oak, concrete and steel make up the limited repertoire of materials and finishes that define the unassuming nature of this home.

Bewegung und Sichtachsen kennzeichnen diese Raumkomposition, die einem zweigeschossigen Haus im „Stick Style" am Stadtrand von San Francisco eine dritte Etage zufügt. Die neue Etage ist ein offener Raum, den sich Bibliothek, Küche, Wohn- und Esszimmer teilen, während auf den anderen beiden Etagen das Hauptschlafzimmer sowie die Kinderzimmer liegen. Die neue Raumführung ist durch eine 15-m lange Betonwand bestimmt, die den Servicebereich verbindet. Charakterisiert werden die Räume durch die für Böden verwendeten Materialien, die Deckenhöhen, Wandstärken und tragenden Säulen. Die Wahl der Materialien und Oberflächenstrukturen beschränkt sich auf Eiche, Beton und Stahl, die für den schlichten Charakter des Hauses steht.

Completion date: **2001**

Mouvement et vision caractérisent cette composition spatiale, ajoutant un troisième niveau à une maison en bois de deux étages de la banlieue de San Francisco. L'ajout comporte une pièce de séjour/repas/cuisine et une bibliothèque partageant un espace unique. Les deux étages abritent la chambre principale et celles des enfants. Le nouveau système de circulation naît d'un mur de béton de 15 m alignant les aires de services. Les matériaux définissent les pièces de la hauteur des plafonds à la surface des sols, des murs épais aux colonnes structurelles. Chêne, béton et acier composent la palette limitée de matériaux et de finitions définissant l'humilité du foyer.

Movimiento y visión caracterizan esta composición de espacios formada por un tercer nivel añadido a una casa adosada de dos pisos de las afueras de San Francisco. La nueva planta aloja salón comedor, cocina y biblioteca en un espacio único compartido; los otros dos pisos contienen el dormitorio principal y los de los niños. El nuevo sistema de circulación viene dictado por un muro de hormigón de 15 m que alinea las áreas de servicio. Las habitaciones se definen por los materiales del suelo, la altura de los techos, el grosor de las paredes y columnas estructurales. La limitada paleta de materiales y acabados –roble, hormigón y acero–, dota a la casa de un aire discreto.

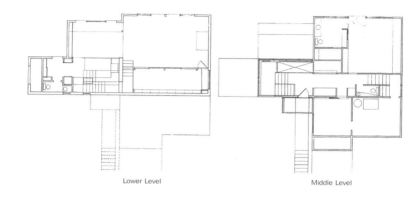

Lower Level

Middle Level

Ward
Residence

LINDY SMALL
lsmallarch@aol.com

Originally designed by the Bay Area architect Henry Hill in the late 1940s, this house received much acclaim for its modernist ideas of horizontality, continuity of spaces and expressive structural system. The contemporary architect Lindy Small was hired to renovate the dining room, kitchen, entrance and bathroom according to the logic of the original house, where light, texture and color play important roles. A common wall was created to link the dining area and the kitchen, and translucent glass partitions were introduced to separate the different areas. Materials like mahogany, glass, slate and stainless steel were used to update both the look and the feel of the home.

Dieses ursprünglich von Henry Hill, dem Architekten des Bay Area, in den späten 1940er Jahren entworfene Haus fand starken Beifall für zukunftsweisende Ideen von Horizontalität, Raumkontinuität und sichtbarem Tragsystem. Die zeitgenössische Architektin Lindy Small erhielt den Auftrag zur Neugestaltung von Esszimmer, Küche, Eingangsbereich und Badezimmer im Sinne der Logik des ursprünglichen Hauses, in dem Licht, Oberflächenstruktur und Farbe eine wichtige Rolle spielen. Eine neue gemeinsame Wand verbindet Essbereich und Küche, zusätzliche durchsichtige Glastrennwände grenzen die einzelnen Bereiche ab. Durch Einsatz von Materialien wie Mahagoni, Glas, Schiefer und Edelstahl wurden Aussehen und Ausstrahlung des Hauses der heutigen Zeit angepasst.

Completion date: **2000**

Design original de la fin des années 1940 d'un architecte de la Baie, Henry Hill, cette maison fut reconnue pour ses idées modernistes d'horizontalité, de continuité des espaces et son structuralisme explicite. L'architecte contemporaine Lindy Small devait rénover la salle à manger, la cuisine, l'entrée et le bain dans la logique originelle : lumières, textures et couleurs jouaient un rôle important. Un mur commun est né pour relier les aires de repas et de cuisine et des partitions vitrées ont été introduites pour le compartimentage. L'acajou, le verre, l'ardoise et l'acier inox actualisent l'aspect et les sensations de la demeure.

Diseñada por el arquitecto de Bay Area Henry Hill a finales de la década de 1940, esta casa destacó por su innovador concepto de la horizontalidad, la continuidad de espacios y un sistema estructural manifiesto. La arquitecta contemporánea Lindy Small recibió el encargo de reformar el comedor, la cocina, la entrada y el baño respetando la lógica de la casa original, en que la luz, la textura y el color tenían un papel importante. Así creó una pared común para delimitar comedor y cocina, e introdujo particiones de cristal traslúcido para separar áreas. Materiales como la caoba, el cristal, la pizarra y el acero inoxidable actualizan el ambiente de la casa.

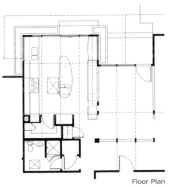

Floor Plan

Kohler Residence

ZACK/DE VITO ARCHITECTURE INC.
jim@zackdevito.com

Located at the edge of San Francisco's culturally diverse Mission District, this residential project is a modernist response to the context and unique character of the city's long, narrow construction lots. Its form follows a simple model: a narrow four-story service and vertical circulation corridor flanked by a wider living volume. This main volume is accentuated by high spaces and warm finishes, while an inner core comprising a gently curving composition of wood and plaster walls defines the fireplace and cabinets and connects the main living spaces. The different areas in the interior are set off by the details of the finishing: the living area features bamboo, glass and wood, while the service section is finished with colder slate tiles and steel.

Dieses Haus am Rande des kulturell vielfältigen Mission Districts von San Francisco ist eine moderne Antwort auf Kontext und einzigartigen Charakter der langen, schmalen Grundstücke der Stadt. Seine Form folgt einem einfachen Schema: Ein schmaler, vierstöckiger Flur als vertikale Geschossverbindung wird von einem geräumigen Wohnbereich flankiert. Hohe Räume und warme Oberflächengestaltungen setzen Akzente im Hauptbaukörper, während der Baukern – eine sanft geschwungene Komposition aus Holz und verputzten Wänden – Kamin und Schränke definiert und die Hauptwohnbereiche miteinander verbindet. Innen hebt die Oberflächengestaltung die Räume voneinander ab: es dominieren Bambus, Glas und Holz, während der Flur in kühlerem Schiefer und Stahl ausgeführt ist.

Completion date: **2002**

À la lisière de Mission district, quartier de diversité culturelle, ce projet résidentiel est une réponse moderniste au contexte et au caractère unique des terrains étroits et longitudinaux de la ville. Il respecte un diagramme simple : un couloir de circulation étroit et vertical de quatre niveaux flanqué d'un large volume à vivre. Ce volume est accentué par de hauts espaces et des finitions chaudes. Le noyau intérieur s'habille de douces courbes en bois, des murs platrés marquant cheminée et mobilier et connecte les espaces de vie. Détails et finitions intérieurs soulignent les aires distinctives. Le séjour s'affiche en bambou, verre et bois, les parties utilitaires optant pour l'ardoise et l'acier, moins chaleureux.

Esta residencia de las afueras del multicultural Mission District de San Francisco es una respuesta moderna al contexto y carácter único de la ciudad con sus construcciones largas y estrechas. Su forma sigue un diagrama simple: una angosta área de servicios repartida entre cuatro plantas y un corredor vertical, flanqueados por una amplia sala. Este volumen principal se acentúa por espacios altos y cálidos acabados, mientras que el núcleo interior central, con una suave composición curva de paredes de madera y yeso, delimita el hogar y una zona de armarios/estanterías, y conecta entre sí las diferentes áreas de la sala. Los detalles y acabados en bambú, cristal y madera diferencian las zonas de estar de los espacios funcionales decorados con frías baldosas de pizarra y con acero.

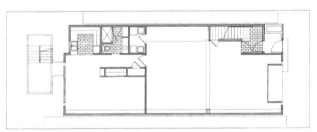

First Floor

Second Floor

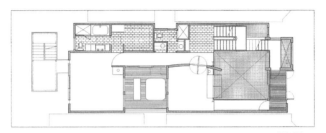

Third Floor

Vonstein Apartment

Craig Steely Architecture
craigsteely@craigsteel.com

This apartment, renovated for a couple who divide their time between Germany and California, sits on top of Telegraph Hill at the same level as the 30th floor of the Transamerica skyscraper. Despite the stunning views provided by the tall windows, the rear half of the apartment was deprived of daylight. Pivoting stainless-steel panels, California walnut and painted wood brightened up the rear rooms, while a steel-and-glass staircase enhanced the flow of light. The upper floor boasts an observation platform and a five-foot sculptural lamp made of blown glass and fiberglass–the architect's design was inspired by the process used to shape a surfboard.

Dieses für ein abwechselnd in Deutschland und Kalifornien lebendes Paar renovierte Apartment liegt auf dem Telegraph Hill, auf derselben Höhe wie das 30. Stockwerk des Transamerica-Hochhauses. Trotz des grandiosen Blicks aus den hohen Fenstern wurde dem hinteren Teil des Apartments Tageslicht entzogen. Drehbar gelagerte Edelstahlpaneele, kalifornische Walnuss und gestrichenes Holz brachten Helligkeit in die hinteren Räume, und eine Glas-Stahl-Treppe verbesserte den Lichtfluss. Hauptattraktion im Obergeschoss ist eine Aussichtsplattform und eine ca. 1,5 m hohe Lichtskulptur aus geblasenem Glas und Fiberglas – ein Entwurf des Architekten, der sich von dem bei der Formgebung für Surfbretter angewandten Verfahren inspirieren ließ.

Completion date: **2000**

Rénové pour un couple vivant entre l'Allemagne et la Californie, cet appartement trône au sommet de Telegraph Hill, en vis à vis avec le 30ème étage de la tour Transamerica. Malgré le panorama saisissant offert par les baies vitrées, la moitié du lieu était privée de lumière du jour. Des panneaux d'acier inox pivotants, du noyer de Californie et du bois peint ont égayé ces pièces. Un escalier mêlant acier et verre a augmenté le flux de lumière. Le niveau supérieur offre une plate-forme d'observation et une lampe sculpturale de 1,5 m, en verre soufflé et fibre de verre, inspirée aux architectes par le processus de fabrication des surfs.

Reformado por una pareja que vive entre Alemania y California, este apartamento se asienta en lo alto de la colina Telegraph, a la misma altura que el piso 30 del rascacielos de la Transamerica. A pesar de las grandiosas vistas de sus grandes ventanales, la parte trasera del apartamento carecía de luz natural. Las habitaciones posteriores se aclararon por medio de paneles de acero inoxidable pivotantes, nogal de California y madera pintada, y una escalera de acero y cristal permitió la entrada de la luz. El piso superior luce una plataforma de observación y una escultural lámpara de 1,5 m de cristal soplado y fibra de vidrio, diseñada por el arquitecto e inspirada en una tabla de surf.

First Floor

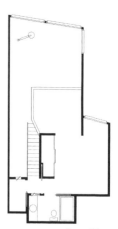

Second Floor

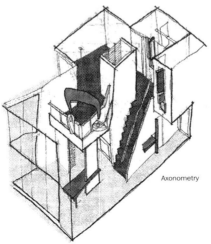

Axonometry

Ghisini/Jacimovic House

CRAIG STEELY ARCHITECTURE
craigsteely@craigsteely.com

This 1920s house in San Francisco's Marina district was renovated inside, but its typically Victorian exterior was preserved. Walking down streets like this one, a passerby would have no inkling of the modern conversions that have taken place inside many of them. Here the original proportions were preserved, although the need for more light and contact with the exterior led to the addition of a floating patio next to the kitchen as well as a viewing platform shrouded in glass on the roof terrace. The architects paid meticulous attention to detail, remodeling every room and adding modern features to match the custom-made furniture in cherry wood, nickel and white Carrara marble.

Diese Haus aus den 1920er Jahren im Marina District von San Francisco wurde im Inneren renoviert, während das typisch viktorianische Äußere erhalten blieb. Ein Straßen wie diese entlangspazierender Passant würde nichts von den modernen Veränderungen ahnen, die im Inneren vorgenommen wurden. Die Proportionen wurden beibehalten, wenngleich aufgrund des Bedürfnisses nach Licht und Kontakt mit außen ein hängender Patio an die Küche angebaut und eine mit Glas verkleidete Aussichtsplattform auf der Dachterrasse errichtet wurde. Die Architekten arbeiteten mit größter Sorgfalt bei der Umgestaltung jedes einzelnen Raumes und fügten moderne Elemente im Einklang mit maßgefertigten Möbeln aus Kirschbaum, Nickel und weißem Carrara-Marmor hinzu.

Completion date: **2001**

Conservant son apparence victorienne typique, une demeure des années 1920 du district de Marina a vu ses intérieurs rénovés. Flânant dans ces rues, un passant ne peut pas s'imaginer les transformations modernes réalisées derrière de nombreuses fenêtres. Les proportions sont demeurées inchangées bien que le besoin de lumière et de contact avec l'extérieur aient impliqué l'ajout d'un patio flottant, vers la cuisine, et d'une plateforme vitrée sur le toit en terrasse, pour le panorama. Les architectes ont traité les détails avec soin, remodelant chaque pièce, ajoutant des détails modernes avec du mobilier personnalisé en cerisier, nickel et marbre de Carrare.

La reforma del interior de esta casa de 1920 del distrito de Marina respetó la fachada típica victoriana. Los paseantes de estas calles jamás podrían intuir las modernas reestructuraciones que se han hecho en la mayoría de las casas. Las proporciones se mantuvieron, aunque la necesidad de más luz y contacto con el exterior llevó a añadir un patio flotante junto a la cocina y una plataforma recubierta de cristal sobre la azotea. Los arquitectos cuidaron con mimo la remodelación de todas las habitaciones, y las decoraron con toques modernos y muebles hechos a medida en madera de cerezo, níquel y mármol de Carrara blanco.

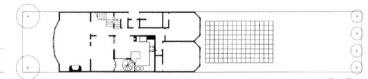

Floor Plan

Fong/Rodríguez House

CRAIG STEELY ARCHITECTURE
craigsteely@craigsteely.com

The client—a writer and journalist—wanted a flexible space in which to live, work and entertain that would respond to the site's stunning views and offer the sensation of being open to the exterior. The living area was placed on the top floor to enjoy the views of the city, while the middle floor has a flexible layout of bedrooms, a writing studio and gallery arranged around sliding cherry wood walls, a glass-treaded staircase and two distinctly colored bathrooms. A stainless-steel rimmed circle eight feet in diameter, cut into the roof of the upper floor balcony, allows in an oval splash of sunlight that moves as the day advances, like a huge sundial.

Der Auftraggeber wünschten sich einen flexiblen Raum zum Wohnen, Arbeiten und Empfangen von Gästen, der dem überwältigenden Ausblick des Grundstücks gerecht würde und sich nach außen öffnete. Der Wohnbereich wurde im obersten Geschoss untergebracht, damit das Stadtpanorama genossen werden kann, während die mittlere Etage in flexibler Anordnung um Schiebewände aus Kirschholz herum Schlafzimmer, ein Schreibzimmer und die Galerie aufnimmt, eine Glasstufentreppe und zwei Bäder. Durch eine edelstahlgefasste, in das Balkondach des Obergeschosses geschnittene runde Öffnung von ca. 2,5 m Durchmesser fällt Sonnenlicht, das sich wie bei einer riesigen Sonnenuhr im Laufe des Tages fortbewegt.

Completion date: **2002**

Le client, écrivain et journaliste, souhaitaient un espace flexible où vivre, travailler et s'amuser : une réponse aux vues fabuleuses du site offrant une sensation d'ouverture sur l'extérieur. Le séjour est monté au sommet pour jouir du panorama sur la ville, le niveau médian accueillant un agencement évolutif de chambres, atelier d'écriture et galerie autour de parois coulissantes en cerisier, d'un escalier pavé de verre et de deux bains aux couleurs distinctes. Un puit de lumière cerclé d'acier inox de 2,5 m dans le toit du balcon supérieur projette un ovale ensoleillé se mouvant avec la progression du jour : un immense cadran solaire.

El cliente, un escritor y periodista, quería un espacio flexible en el que vivir y trabajar, que ofreciese espectaculares vistas y la sensación de encontrarse en el exterior. El salón está en el piso superior para poder contemplar la panorámica de la ciudad. El piso intermedio aloja una composición flexible de dormitorios, un estudio y una galería formados por paredes corredizas de madera de cerezo, una caja de escalera de cristal y dos baños decorados en colores distintos. Una abertura circular enmarcada en acero inoxidable de 2,5 m de diámetro en el techo del mirador del piso superior ofrece un óvalo de luz que cambia a lo largo del día como si se tratara de un gran reloj de sol.

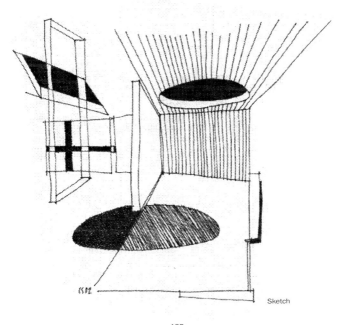

Sketch

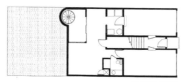

Ground Floor

First Floor

Second Floor

Bernal Heights Residence

ANDRE ROTHBLATT
arothblatt@aol.com

The design of this project, which aims to present an impassive, reserved exterior hiding a more expressive and intimate interior, pays special attention to materials, detail and craftsmanship. The exterior structure is tiered up the slope of the street so as to not overwhelm its lower neighbor down the hill. A staircase made of wenge and Douglas Fir provides the focal point that anchors the main space. An integrated kitchen and dining room features a sandblasted glass tile backdrop, countertops from the company FireSlate and a natural wood closet with an interlocking motif. A splayed maple plywood skylight defines the dining area, where hanging lights hover over the table.

Ziel war es, ein strenges und zurückhaltendes Äußeres sowie ein ausdrucksstärkeres und intimeres Inneres widerzuspiegeln, wobei Materialien, Detailausführungen und handwerklicher Verarbeitung besondere Beachtung geschenkt wurde. Die Außenstruktur folgt der Neigung der Straße, sodass keine Dominanz gegenüber dem kleineren Nachbarbau entsteht. Eine Treppe aus Wenge und Douglastanne bildet den absoluten Mittelpunkt im Inneren und fixiert den Hauptraum. Das Aussehen der Wohnküche wird bestimmt von einem sandgestrahlten Glasstehbord, Ablagen der Firma FireSlate und einem Schrank aus naturbelassenem Holz. Die Deckenbeleuchtung aus Ahornfurnier und Hängelampen definieren den Essbereich.

Completion date: **2002**

Le concept du projet devait dépeindre un extérieur stoïque et réservé et un intérieur plus expressif et intime, avec une attention spéciale aux matériaux, aux détails et au savoir faire. La structure extérieure est décalée au-dessus de la rue afin de ne pas envahir le voisin du bas. Un escalier en Wenge et en Douglas vert devient l'attrait central des intérieurs, ancrant l'espace principal. Une cuisine intégrée et une salle à manger proposent un dosseret en verre sablé, des plans de travail de FireSlate et une armoire en bois naturel avec un motif entrelacé. Un plafond évasé en érable contreplaqué définit l'aire de repas où des mobiles de lumière planent sur la table.

Este proyecto intentó crear un exterior austero y reservado, y un interior más expresivo e íntimo, prestando especial atención al material, a los detalles y al trabajo artesano. La estructura exterior se adapta escalonada a la pendiente de la calle como si no quisiera avasallar al vecino de abajo. Una escalera de madera de wenge y pino de Oregón veteado es el foco central del interior, y sirve de anclaje al espacio principal. En la cocina comedor destaca el frontal alicatado con cristal mateado al chorro de arena, las encimeras de FireSlate y un armario de madera natural con un motivo unificador. Una claraboya biselada de arce contrachapado define el área del comedor, sobre cuya mesa pende una lámpara colgante.

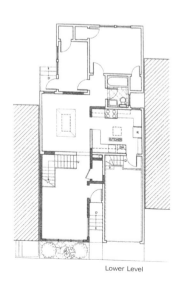

Lower Level

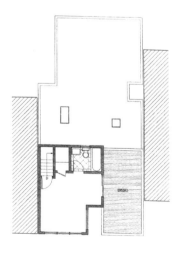

Upper Level

**Magnolia
Row**

DAVID BAKER + PARTNERS
michellepeckham@dbarchitect.com

The West Clawson area, long populated by artists and craftsmen, is home to a varied, highly creative community that have settled in lofts and artists' studios. This project, one of a series of townhouses by David Baker + Partners, is a cross between an urban loft and a residential home. Large, open living areas span the main floor, with open-riser wooden stairways linking these to the more private bedrooms. The open-plan kitchen is equipped with stainless steel gas stoves, granite counters and maple closets. Hydronic heating, energy-efficient water heaters and state-of-the-art electronic equipment mean that these townhouses are not only well designed but also ecologically and technologically advanced.

Das von Künstlern bewohnte Viertel von West Clawson ist Heimatstadt für eine kreative Gemeinschaft mit ihren Lofts und Ateliers. Dieses zu einer Reihe von Stadthäusern von David Baker + Partner gehörende Projekt ist ein Hybrid aus städtischem Loft und Wohnhaus. Große offene Wohnbereiche überspannen die Hauptetage und werden über Holztreppen ohne Setzstufen mit den privateren Schlafzimmern verbunden. Die durchgehende Küche ist mit Edelstahlgasherd, Granitablagen und Ahornschränken ausgestattet. Energiesparende Heizung, hochleistungsfähige Warmwasserbereiter und neueste elektronische Ausstattung sorgen bei diesen Stadthäusern nicht nur für gutes Design, sondern auch für Umweltfreundlichkeit und Fortschrittlichkeit .

Completion date: **2003**

Peuplée d'artistes et d'artisans durant des décennies, West Clawson accueille divers groupes d'individus et un communauté créative dans ses lofts et ateliers d'artistes. Élément d'une série d'hôtels particuliers de David Baker + Partners, ce projet est l'hybride d'un loft urbain et d'une maison résidentielle. Des aires de séjour ouvertes peuplent l'étage principal, un escalier de bois ajouré les reliant aux chambres intimes. Le plan ouvert de la cuisine comprend un four à gaz en inox, des plans de travail en granite et des armoires en érable. Chauffage hydronique économe à air pulsé, chaudières à eau efficientes, appareils électroniques de pointe : ces résidences sont écologiques, technologiquement en avance et bien conçues.

Habitada por artistas y artesanos durante décadas, la zona de West Clawson ha sido el hogar de gentes variopintas y una comunidad marcadamente creativa que vive en lofts y talleres. Este proyecto, uno de los muchos de David Baker + Partners, es un híbrido entre un loft urbano y una casa residencial. Amplias y diáfanas áreas de salón ocupan el piso principal y una escalera de madera sin contrahuellas las comunica con los dormitorios. La cocina, de concepción abierta, está equipada con fuegos de gas de acero inoxidable, encimeras de granito y armarios de madera de arce. La calefacción hidrónica, calentadores de agua de alto rendimiento y lo último en equipamiento electrónico hacen de ésta una casa ecológica, tecnológicamente avanzada y, desde luego, bien diseñada.

First Floor

Second Floor

Third Floor

Ritch Zoe Studios

SANTOS PRESCOTT AND ASSOCIATES
bruce@santosprescott.com

A long, narrow concrete warehouse set between two parallel narrow streets was the starting point for this residence/workplace loft in the South of Market district of San Francisco. The building was overhauled to resist earthquakes and a courtyard was cut into the center of the building to introduce light and ventilation into the living space. A double-height level with mezzanines was added to the top of both ends of the building, taking advantage of the existing concrete frame, with multi-pane windows tucked into the pattern created by the original openings. The tenant has made his mark inside with a large, eclectic collection of exotic objects and sculptures.

Ein langes schmales Lagerhaus aus Beton zwischen zwei parallelen engen Straßen ist der Standort für dieses Loft im South-of-Market-Viertel. Das Gebäude wurde erdbebensicher umgebaut, und in die Mitte des Gebäudes wurde ein Innenhof geschnitten um Licht und Frischluft in die Wohnräume zu bringen. Eine Etage von doppelter Höhe mit Zwischengeschossen wurde auf das Gebäude aufgesetzt. Für den Oberbau auf der Straßenseite wurden das existierende Betongerüst genutzt und Sprossenfenster in die von den vorhandenen Öffnungen gebildeten Strukturen eingesetzt. Eine umfangreiche Sammlung ethnischer Kunst und Skulpturen prägen den Charakter dieses Wohnhauses.

Completion date: **1998**

Un entrepôt en béton, long et étroit, entre deux ruelles parallèles accueille ce loft, lieu de vie et de travail, du district de South of Market. L'immeuble a été mis aux normes anti-sismiques et une cour prévue en son centre pour offrir lumière et aération aux espaces de séjour. Une double hauteur en mezzanine a été ajoutée à chaque angle du sommet de l'édifice. Les élévations sur rue reposent sur une structure de béton existante, avec des panneaux vitrés multiples dans les ouvertures existantes. Une vaste collection éclectique d'objets et de sculptures ethniques personnalise la demeure.

Una alargada nave de hormigón entre dos callejones paralelos del distrito de South of Market de San Francisco acoge este loft que sirve de vivienda y lugar de trabajo. El edificio fue reformado para soportar los movimientos sísmicos. Asimismo se construyó un patio en su centro para dotar de luz y ventilación a los espacios habitables. Sobre cada extremo de la nave se añadió un nivel de doble altura mediante estructuras modulares metálicas. Los alzados de la calle se basan en el armazón de hormigón preexistente, y se instalaron ventanales acristalados en los vanos originales. Una ecléctica colección de objetos étnicos y esculturas dan carácter a esta vivienda.

Third Floor

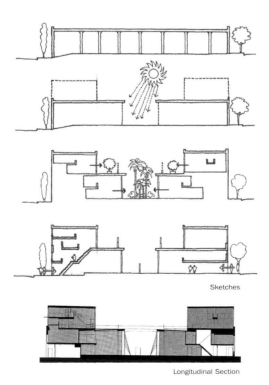

Sketches

Longitudinal Section

**Minott
Residence**

CHARLIE BARNETT ASSOCIATES
jane@charliebarnettassoc.com

A hierarchical division of space defines this residence with spectacular views of the city. The house gradually progresses from the intimate garden level through to a grand living room on the top level. A three-story wood, steel and aluminum staircase set against a glass curtain wall links the lower level office, mid-level entrance and bedrooms with the top-floor living area. Light penetrates through a skylight from which two stories of bookshelves are suspended between aluminum tension rods. A twenty-foot-high shower capped by another skylight is sheathed in soft gray tiles. The project makes a dramatic use of vertical space, capturing the constant variations of the sunlight.

Eine räumliche Hierarchie prägt dieses Wohnhaus mit Sicht auf die Stadt. Die Abstufung erfolgt von der Ebene des Gartens bis zu einem großen Wohnzimmer im Obergeschoss. Eine sich über drei Etagen erstreckende, an eine Glasfassade gelehnte Treppe aus Holz, Stahl und Aluminium verbindet das Büro im Unter-, Eingang und Schlafzimmer im Mittel- und den Wohnbereich im Obergeschoss. Licht dringt durch eine Dachluke, an der über zwei Etagen reichende, zwischen Aluminiumzugstangen befestigte Bücherregale aufgehängt sind. Eine 6 m hohe, von einem weiteren Dachfenster gekrönte Dusche ist in einem weichen Grau gefliest. Das Projekt ist eine lebendige Interpretation des vertikalen Raums und fängt die sich verändernden natürlichen Lichtverhältnisse ein.

Completion date: **2001**

Une hiérarchie d'espaces définit cette résidence aux superbes vues sur la ville. Une échelle graduelle progresse de l'intimité du jardin au grand séjour du dernier étage. Contre une cloison vitrée, un escalier en bois, aluminium et acier de trois niveaux relie l'office du bas, l'entrée et les chambres du milieu et le salon du haut. La lumière pénètre par une claire-voie où sont suspendus deux niveaux de bibliothèque, entre des barres de tension aluminées. Une douche de 6 m couverte d'une autre claire-voie est gainée de douces tuiles grises. Le projet utilise spectaculairement l'espace vertical, capturant les constantes variations de lumière naturelle.

Esta casa con vistas sobre la ciudad se define por una jerarquía de espacios que ascienden gradualmente desde el íntimo jardín hasta una enorme sala situada en el nivel superior. La escalera de madera, acero y aluminio, sustentada contra una pared de cristal, comunica el despacho del nivel inferior, la entrada y los dormitorios de la planta intermedia con el salón del piso de arriba. La luz penetra por una claraboya de la que penden atornilladas dos estanterías de libros. Coronada por otra claraboya, el espacio de la ducha, con una altura de 6 m, está recubierto con azulejos de un suave tono gris. El proyecto hace un uso teatral del espacio vertical para captar las constantes variaciones de la luz natural.

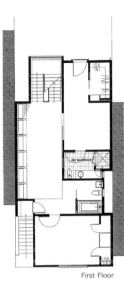

First Floor

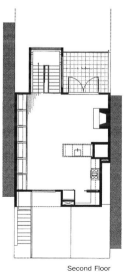

Second Floor

Lloyd Loft

AIDLIN DARLING DESIGN LLP
ja@aidlin-darling-design.com

The design of this loft conversion revolved around three major challenges tackled by the architects. The first involved opening up a series of dark and cluttered spaces by removing walls and adding skylights and a two-story glass light fixture. The second was to create a gallery-like backdrop to display the client's significant art collection. Finally, the third aim was to integrate most of the functional services in a series of built-in closets, replete with a host of high-tech installations that control the lighting, entertainment and sound systems throughout the loft. When these functional elements are not in use, their presence is sculptural but discrete.

Im Mittelpunkt des Entwurfs für diesen Loftausbau standen drei von den Architekten zu lösende Hauptaufgaben. Die erste bestand im Öffnen einer Reihe dunkler, unübersichtlicher Räume durch Entfernen von Wänden und Einbau von Dachfenstern sowie eines über zwei Etagen reichenden gläsernen Lichtfängers. Die zweite sah die Schaffung einer galerieartigen Kulisse für die Kunstsammlung des Kunden vor. Die dritte beinhaltete die Integration eines Großteils der funktionalen Elemente in einer Reihe von Einbauschränken mit einer Vielzahl von Hightechanlagen zur Kontrolle der Beleuchtungs-, Unterhaltungs- und Tonanlagen im gesamten Loft. Bei Nichtgebrauch wirken diese funktionalen Elemente skulpturenhaft und zurückhaltend.

Completion date: **2002**

Le design de ce loft rénové gravite autour des trois objectifs essentiels des architectes. Le premier visait à ouvrir une série d'espaces sombres et confus en retirant les murs pour ajouter des claires-voies et une paroi en verre soufflé de deux niveaux. Le second devait offrir une toile de fond de galerie pour présenter l'importante collection du client. Enfin, le troisième objectif voulait intégrer l'essentiel du programme fonctionnel en une série de réduits encastrés, contenant nombreuses d'appareils high-tech pour contrôler la lumière et le système audio-visuel du loft. Ces éléments fonctionnels, quand ils ne sont pas utilisés, apparaissent sculpturels et sobres.

Los arquitectos responsables de la remodelación de este loft se marcaron tres objetivos principales. El primero fue abrir una serie de espacios oscuros y opresivos eliminando tabiques, y añadiendo claraboyas y una cavidad acristalada de dos pisos de altura. El segundo objetivo fue crear una galería que sirviera de telón de fondo para exponer la significativa colección de arte del cliente. Finalmente, se pretendió integrar la mayoría de los elementos funcionales en una serie de armarios empotrados que contuvieran las numerosas instalaciones de control de la iluminación y los aparatos de entretenimiento y sonido de todo el loft. De esta forma cuando no se utilizan, su presencia es escultural y sobria.

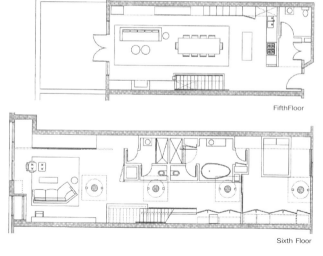

FifthFloor

Sixth Floor

The Castro

MICHAEL MULLIN ARCHITECT, LTD.
mmullinarch@earthlink.net

The owner of this apartment wished to turn the cluttered kitchen and bathroom into light, open, expansive spaces. As in many Victorian homes, this building was cut off from its backyard by the addition of utility rooms. In this case, the architect remodelled the pantry and laundry porch spaces and integrated them into the kitchen, housing the various facilities in custom-made closets. The dining area was defined by the corner windows and high tarred ceiling of the former porch and pantry. The bathroom design is modern but finished with traditional materials, and an open shower gives the sensation of a larger space. The variety of form and finish makes each room spatially and functionally distinct.

Wunsch des Besitzers dieser Wohnung war Küche und Bad in helle, offene und großzügige Räume zu verwandeln. Wie viele viktorianische Häuser war auch dieses durch Hauswirtschaftsräume vom Hinterhof abgeschnitten. Der Architekt entschied sich für den Umbau der Waschküche und der Vorratskammer und deren Eingliederung in die Küche, wobei er maßgefertigte Schränke für die genannten Einrichtungen vorsah. Der Essbereich erhielt seine Gestalt durch Eckfenster und die hohe Decke des ehemaligen Vorbaus und der Vorratskammer. Das Badezimmerdesign ist modern, verwendete jedoch traditionelle Materialien, und eine kabinenlose Dusche vergrößert den Raum. Die Form- und Oberflächenausführungen machen aus jedem Raum etwas Einzigartiges.

Completion date: **2001**

Le propriétaire du logement voulait transformer une cuisine et un bain encombrés en généreux espaces ouverts et clairs. Comme nombreuses de maisons victoriennes, celle-ci était coupée de la cour par des espaces utilitaires. Ici, l'architecte a remanié le porche de l'office et de la buanderie pour les intégrer à la cuisine, abritant les fonctions dans des armoires sur mesure. Les fenêtres d'angle et le haut plafond des anciens porche et office définissent l'aire repas. Le design du bain est moderne mais sa finition traditionnelle et une douche sans rebord donne la sensation d'un espace plus vaste. Formes et finitions variées singularisent l'espace et la fonction des chambres.

El propietario de este piso deseaba transformar la cocina y el baño en espacios luminosos, amplios y abiertos. Como en muchas residencias victorianas, ésta se veía privada de su patio trasero por una recocina adicional. En este caso, el arquitecto remodeló la despensa y el lavadero y los integró en la cocina, encerrando los diferentes elementos en armarios hechos a medida. El área del comedor quedó definida por los ventanales angulares y el alto techo abuhardillado de la despensa y entrada originales. El diseño del baño es moderno pero acabado con materiales tradicionales, y la ducha abierta ofrece una sensación de mayor amplitud. La variedad en la forma y los acabados de cada habitación las hacen espacial y funcionalmente únicas.

Previous Floor Plan

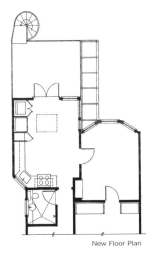

New Floor Plan

Liberty Hill

MICHAEL MULLIN ARCHITECT, LTD.
mmullinarch@earthlink.net

The main aim of this conversion of a Victorian house was the creation of stronger connections between the house and the garden. The old enclosed kitchen and utility rooms were torn down and in their place a new kitchen was built, with a media room above it. The high kitchen windows look out on the terraced gardens and the media room has a new shady balcony, reached by a curved wall of windows with a 180-degree view of the landscaped garden. The Alaskan yellow cedar beneath the overhanging roof gives warm color, natural texture and a sense of enclosure and intimacy to the exterior space and the otherwise formal facade. Inside, an interesting art collection adorns the home.

Verbindungen zwischen Haus und Garten waren das Hauptziel beim Umbau dieses viktorianischen Hauses. Die geschlossene Küche nebst Hauswirtschaftsräumen wurde abgerissen und eine neue Küche mit einem Medienzimmer darüber errichtet. Die hohen Küchenfenster geben den Blick auf die terrassenförmig angelegten Gärten frei, während das Medienzimmer, dessen gewölbte Fensterwand den Blick im 180° Winkel über den Garten schweifen lässt, auf einen schattigen Balkon führt. Die Nootka-Scheinzeder neben dem überhängenden Dach schafft einen warmen Ton, natürlichen Hintergrund und Gefühl von Abgeschlossenheit und Intimität gegenüber dem Außenraum und einer strengen Fassade. Im Inneren schmückt eine interessante Kunstsammlung das Haus.

Completion date: **1996**

Renforcer le lien entre la maison et le jardin était le but principal de cette réforme victorienne. Cuisine et pièces utilitaires ont été mises à bas pour recréer une nouvelle cuisine dotée, au-dessus, d'une salle médias. Les baies vitrées de la cuisine donnent sur les jardins en terrasse et la salle médias sur un balcon ombré, dont le mur de fenêtres arqué offre une vue à 180 degrés sur le jardin paysager. Le cèdre jaune d'Alaska, sous le toit suspendu, apporte des tons chaleureux, une texture naturelle et un sens de l'intimité à l'espace extérieur et la façade sinon formelle. À l'intérieur, une collection artistique d'intérêt orne la demeure.

El objetivo principal de la remodelación de este edificio victoriano fue lograr una mayor conexión entre la casa y el jardín. Las antiguas cocina y recocina cerradas se suprimieron; en su lugar se construyó una nueva cocina con altas ventanas abiertas al jardín, y una sala para escuchar música y ver la televisión que da a un nuevo balcón protegido del sol, con una arcada acristalada que ofrece una vista de 180 grados sobre el jardín. La madera de cedro amarrillo de Alaska bajo el saliente del tejado da un color cálido, textura natural y una sensación de recogimiento e intimidad al espacio exterior, y logra que la fachada pierda su aspecto demasiado formal. Dentro, una interesante colección de arte adorna la casa.

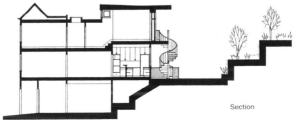

Section

185

Potrero Hill

MICHAEL MULLIN ARCHITECT, LTD.
mmullinarch@earthlink.net

This renovation converted two living units into a comfortable family home. This Victorian house acquired various additions over the last century, to the detriment of its visual unity. In order to open up the house, the interior spaces were defined more by closets, windows and varying ceiling heights than by walls. The roof was raised to make the loft serve for living purposes, and both sides were opened up by windows with panoramic views of the exterior. The remnants of design elements from the house's past combine with the integrated modern details to give a great sense of depth and character.

Bei dieser Renovierung wurden zwei Wohneinheiten zu einem komfortablen Einfamilienhaus zusammengefasst. Das viktorianische Haus hatte im Laufe des letzten Jahrhunderts durch zahlreiche Ausbauten seine architektonische Einheit verloren. Zur Öffnung des Hauses wurden die Innenräume eher durch Wandschränke, Fenster und unterschiedliche Deckenhöhen als durch Wände definiert. Das Dach wurde angehoben um Wohnraum zu schaffen und beide Seiten erhielten Fenster mit Panoramablick auf die Umgebung. Die mit den Spuren von Gestaltungselementen aus der Vergangenheit des Hauses verbundenen modernen Details verleihen dem Haus einen starken Ausdruck von Tiefe und Charakter.

Completion date: **2001**

Cette rénovation associe deux unités en un seul foyer familial confortable. Fruit d'ajouts au siècle dernier, la demeure victorienne avait perdu son intégrité conceptuelle. Afin d'ouvrir le lieu, les espaces intérieurs ont été définis par le mobilier, les fenêtres et les hauteurs de plafond et non par des murs. L'élévation du toit a rendu le loft apte au séjour et les deux côtés ont été ouverts par des baies aux vues panoramiques. Les traces d'éléments de design de son évolution et ses détails modernes intégrés confèrent à la demeure son sens de la profondeur et sa personnalité.

Esta reforma aunó dos espacios independientes en una única y confortable residencia unifamiliar. Con las continuas remodelaciones del último siglo, este edificio victoriano había perdido su integridad de diseño. Para abrir la casa al exterior, los espacios interiores se redefinieron por medio de armarios, ventanas y techos de diferentes alturas en lugar de por tabiques. Se levantó el tejado para aprovechar el desván como salón, y en ambos costados se abrieron ventanas con vistas panorámicas al exterior. La pervivencia de elementos de diseño de la evolución de la casa junto con algunos detalles modernos crea una sensación de carácter y profundidad.

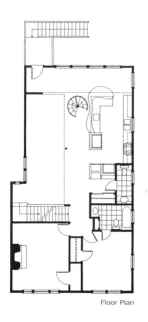

Floor Plan

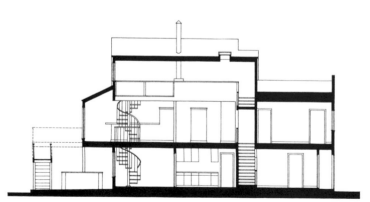

Transversal Section

Lower Pacific Heights

MICHAEL MULLIN ARCHITECT, LTD.
mmullinarch@earthlink.net

This project involved the construction of a new kitchen for a gourmet client who wished to have both a kitchen apt for a team of chefs and space for guests keen on gastronomy. The new kitchen uses vertical proportions and solid stone finishes to create a formal and almost rustic feel, in contrast with the surrounding modern interiors. A large island marks the center of the space, while the wooden oven is the special attraction. The new dining room bar and serving hatch make it easier to attend to guests. High doors allow light into the kitchen, softening the effect of the house's long axis. The layout provides a comfortable, functional and urbane setting for cooking and hosting dinner parties.

Der Auftraggeber für dieses Projekt wünschte den Bau einer neuen Küche für mehrere Köche sowie Raum für Gäste mit Freude am Kochen. In der Küche dominieren vertikale Proportionen und Oberflächen in Naturstein, wodurch eine strenge und nahezu rustikale Atmosphäre entsteht, die mit dem sie umgebenden modernen Interieur kontrastiert. Eine lange Insel markiert die Mitte des Raumes, während der Holzbackofen eine besondere Attraktion darstellt. Esstheke und Durchreiche erleichtern das Servieren. Hohe Türen bringen Licht in die Küche und lindern die Dominanz der Längsachse des Hauses. Das Arrangement schafft einen angenehmen, funktionalen und urbanen Rahmen zum Kochen und Essen.

Completion date: **2002**

Ce projet impliquait la construction d'une nouvelle cuisine pour un client gourmet souhaitant la proposer à des chefs et invités férus de gastronomie. La nouvelle cuisine emploie proportions verticales et finitions substantielles en pierre pour créer un effet formel quasi rustique en regard des intérieurs modernes. Un vaste îlot marque le centre de l'espace avec un four à bois en attraction spéciale. Le nouveau bar et le passe-plat de la salle à manger facilitent le service. De hautes portes illuminent la cuisine, adoucissant l'influence de l'axe de la maison. L'ensemble offre un cadre confortable, fonctionnel et urbain pour la cuisine et les soirées.

Este cliente gourmet quería una cocina con suficientes facilidades y espacio como para poder ser utilizada por varios chefs y huéspedes aficionados al arte de la gastronomía. La nueva cocina presenta proporciones verticales y sustanciales acabados en piedra que crean una atmósfera formal y casi rústica en comparación con los modernos interiores colindantes. Una gran isla marca el centro del espacio, mientras que el horno de madera es la principal atracción. El bar y la ventanilla del comedor facilitan el servicio. Las altas puertas dan luz a la cocina y suavizan la presión de los largos ejes de la casa. La decoración crea una atmósfera confortable, funcional y urbana para cocinar y cenar entre amigos.

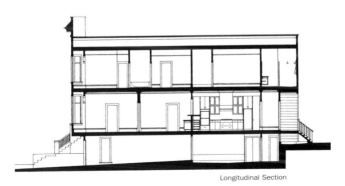

Longitudinal Section

Elsie Street Residence

JERRY VEVERKA
jerry@veverka.com

The owners of this private residence, located on a steeply sloping urban lot, wanted a New York-style loft with its own private garden. Space and light are the primary elements of the design. The main living space, which includes the lounge, kitchen/dining room and master bedroom, is situated to receive the maximum possible light, and the level below contains a study and guest bedroom just above the garage. The main bedroom floats in a light and airy volume, set at an odd angle to emphasize its context within a larger space. The house was designed to meet a stringent set of community-generated guidelines and was intended to blend naturally into the neighborhood.

Die Besitzer dieses auf einem stufenweise abfallenden Grundstück gelegenen Hauses wünschten sich ein Loft im New Yorker Stil mit eigenem Garten. Raum und Licht sind die Grundelemente des Entwurfs. Der Wohnraum, zu dem Salon, Küche/Esszimmer und ein großes Schlafzimmer gehören, wurde so angelegt, dass er ein Maximum an Licht erhält. Die Etage darunter beherbergt ein Atelier und ein Gästezimmer über der Garage. Das Schlafzimmer schwebt in einem hellen und luftigen Baukörper mit einem ungewöhnlichen Winkel, der den Kontext zum umgebenden Raum betont. Ausschlaggebend für den Entwurf waren eine Reihe strenger Richtlinien der Gemeinde sowie die Absicht, eine natürliche Einpassung in die Nachbarschaft zu erreichen.

Completion date: **1992**

Les propriétaires de cette résidence, située sur une parcelle en pente prononcée, désiraient un loft à la new-yorkaise avec jardin privatif. Espace et lumière sont les éléments principaux du design. L'espace de vie principal, incluant le séjour, la pièce repas/cuisine et la chambre principale, est disposé pour recevoir le maximum de lumière. Le niveau inférieur contient un atelier et une chambre d'invité sur le garage. La chambre principale flotte dans un volume lumineux et aéré, son angularité étrange souligne son contexte dans un espace plus vaste. Le design devait répondre à des règles strictes de directives communautaires et a été pensé pour se fondre dans le voisinage.

Los propietarios de esta residencia privada, localizada en un solar urbano escalonado, deseaban un loft de estilo neoyorquino con un jardín particular. Espacio y luz son los elementos primarios del diseño. El área de vivienda principal, que incluye un salón, una cocina comedor y una suite, está orientada de forma que pueda recibir la mayor cantidad de luz posible, y el nivel inferior contiene un estudio con una habitación para huéspedes encima del garaje. El dormitorio principal flota en un volumen luminoso y diáfano con una extraña perspectiva que enfatiza la amplitud del espacio. La casa fue diseñada respetando la severa normativa municipal y pretendió no desentonar con el carácter del barrio.

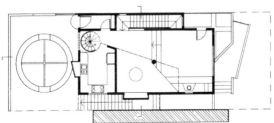

Second Floor

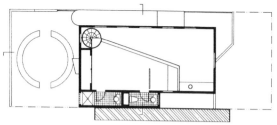

Loft Level

Zircon Place Residence

VEVERKA ARCHITECTS

jerry@veverka.com

This intervention involved a major overhaul of a 1960s residence with sweeping views of the city. The roof was raised to allow the insertion of a new loft-style office/bedroom and bathroom. A light metal bridge and spiral staircase links the loft to the main level. The kitchen was enlarged and two bedrooms of equal size were transformed into a large master suite and a smaller guest bedroom. The wooden shingle structure, distinctive pitched ceiling and pale interiors give this home its character. A series of sliding mahogany panels and bookcases provides the unifying element in the overall design.

Es handelt sich um den umfassenden Umbau eines Hauses aus den 1960er Jahren mit Panoramablick über die Stadt. Das Dach wurde zum Einbau eines loftartigen Büro/Schlafzimmer und Bad angehoben. Über eine leichte Metallbrücke und eine spiralförmige Treppe ist der Loft mit der Hauptetage verbunden. Die Küche wurde vergrößert, und aus zwei gleich großen Schlafzimmern entstanden ein großes Schlafzimmer sowie ein kleineres Gästezimmer. Die Holzschindelstruktur, die einzigartige hohe Decke und helle Innenräume charakterisieren dieses Haus. Eine Reihe von Schiebepaneelen und Bücherregalen aus Mahagoni wurde zum verbindenden Element des Gesamtdesigns.

Completion date: **2000**

L'intervention a impliqué la réforme d'une résidence années 1960 aux vues enivrantes sur la ville. Le toit, relevé, a permis d'insérer un nouveau loft bureau/chambre et bain. Un frêle escalier métallique en spirale relie le loft au niveau principal. La cuisine a été agrandie et deux chambres similaires transformées en une vaste suite et une petite chambre d'invité. La structure de bardeau, le toit en pente et les intérieurs clairs caractérisent le lieu. Une série de panneaux et d'étagères en acajou devient l'élément unifiant le design d'ensemble.

Esta casa de la década de 1960 con espectaculares vistas sobre la ciudad se reformó totalmente. El tejado se elevó para poder acondicionar un despacho dormitorio y un baño. Un ligero puente de metal y una escalera en espiral unen el desván con el piso principal. Se amplió la cocina, y dos dormitorios de tamaño similar se transformaron en una amplia suite y una pequeña habitación de invitados. La estructura de tablillas de madera, el techo abuhardillado y los claros interiores caracterizan esta vivienda. Una serie de librerías y paneles de caoba corredizos se convirtieron en el elemento unificador del conjunto del diseño.

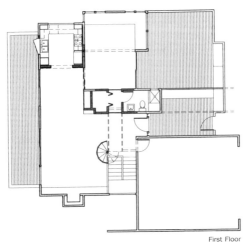

First Floor

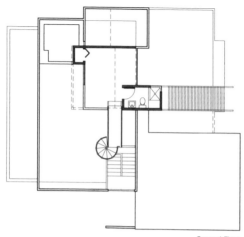

Second Floor

Kalmbach Residence

HOUSE + HOUSE ARCHITECTS
house@ix.netcom.com

This renovation in San Francisco's Marina district transformed a century-old duplex into a contemporary home filled with natural light and rich materials. A new three-story addition was added to the back to create a two-story, loft-like living area and kitchen with a new master suite above. Carefully placed windows and skylights create a sculptured space replete with striking materials, such as bamboo on the floors, steel cable railings on the balconies and zinc around the fireplace. Old industrial fixtures are mixed with new elements throughout. Maple cabinets, antique tables, classic furniture and an eclectic art collection illustrate the owner's diverse tastes.

Mit der Renovierung wurde ein zweistöckiges Haus aus dem letzten Jahrhundert im Jachthafenviertel von San Francisco in ein zeitgenössisches Heim voller Tageslicht und edler Materialien verwandelt. Ein neuer dreigeschossiger Anbau wurde an der Rückseite angefügt, um einen zweigeschossigen, offenen Wohnbereich mit Küche und großem Schlafzimmer darüber zu schaffen. Mit Bedacht platzierte Fenster und Dachluken lassen einen sorgsam gestalteten Raum entstehen mit auffälligen Materialien wie Bambus für den Boden, Stahlseilen an den Geländern und Zink am Kamin. Altes wird durchgängig mit Neuem kombiniert. Ahornschränke, antike Tische, klassische Möbel und Kunstwerke bringen den vielfältigen Geschmack des Bewohners zum Ausdruck.

Completion date: **2002**

Cette rénovation du district de la Marina a transformé un duplex centenaire en un foyer moderne empli de lumière naturelle et de matériaux riches. Un ajout de trois étages sur l'arrière a créé une zone de séjour en loft de deux niveaux avec cuisine, et une suite principale au-dessus. Disposées avec soin, fenêtres et claires-voies sculptent l'espace riche en matériaux comme le bambou au sol, les câbles d'acier aux balcons et le zinc de la cheminée. D'anciens éclairages industriels se mêlent aux nouveaux éléments. Placards en érable, tables anciennes, mobilier classique et collection artistique éclectique expriment le goût de l'auteur pour la variété.

Este dúplex centenario del distrito de Marina se transformó en una vivienda contemporánea llena de luz y gran riqueza de materiales. En la parte trasera se incorporó un añadido de tres pisos para crear un área diáfana de dos alturas con un salón y una cocina, y encima una suite. Las ventanas y claraboyas colocadas cuidadosamente crean un espacio escultural subrayado por materiales de fuerte presencia como el bambú del suelo, los cables de acero de las barandillas de los balcones y el zinc que rodea la chimenea. Los elementos industriales se mezclan con detalles modernos. Armarios de arce, mesas antiguas, mobiliario clásico y una ecléctica colección de arte expresan el gusto del propietario por la variedad de estilos.

First Floor

Second Floor

Third Floor

Grandview House

HOUSE + HOUSE ARCHITECTS
house@ix.netcom.com

The Oakland firestorm in 1991 did away with what was supposed to be a remodelling project for a family home. From the ashes, however, rose an opportunity for something new and a chance for the clients to rebuild their lives. The new design resulted in a home geared to feng shui with meaning in every curve, angle and perspective. The rooms are designed to take advantage of the sunrises and sunsets in accordance with the birth dates of the family members. Steel and glass create waves and curves, while stone seems to float and unusually colored wood appears natural. An array of colors and hand-painted surfaces convey the distinctive character of this energy-filled residence.

Die Oakland-Feuersbrunst fegte 1991 hinweg, was der Umbau für ein Eigenheim werden sollte. Die Asche jedoch bot die Gelegenheit für Neues und für die Auftraggeber die Möglichkeit, ihr Leben neu zu gestalten. Das neue Haus basiert auf einem an Feng Shui orientierten Entwurf, bei dem jede Wölbung, jeder Winkel und jede Perspektive ihre Bedeutung hat. Die Räume sind so angelegt, dass sie die Sonnenauf- und Sonnenuntergänge im Zusammenhang mit den Geburtstagen der Familienmitglieder einfangen. Stahl und Glas schaffen Wellen und Wölbungen, Stein fließt und Holz in ungewöhnlichen Farbtönen wirkt naturnah. Eine Vielzahl Farben und handbemalter Oberflächen verleiht diesem energieerfüllten Wohnhaus seinen besonderen Charakters.

Completion date: **1997**

L'incendie d'Oakland de 1991 a emporté ce qui devait être un projet de rénovation pour un foyer familial. Des cendres a jailli une opportunité de nouveauté et une chance pour les clients de reconstruire leurs vies. Le nouveau design de la maison respecte le feng shui, donnant du sens aux courbes, angles et perspectives. Les pièces sont conçues pour bénéficier de l'aube et du crépuscule et liées aux anniversaires des membres de la famille. Acier et verre créent ondes et courbes, la pierre flotte et le bois aux tons rares semble naturel. Une multitude de couleurs et de surfaces peintes à la main exprime le caractère particulier de ce lieu d'énergie.

El incendio de Oakland de 1991 acabó con lo que se suponía era una remodelación de una casa familiar. De entre las cenizas, sin embargo, surgió para los clientes la oportunidad de crear algo nuevo, de reconstruir sus vidas. El nuevo hogar nació a partir de un diseño inspirado en el feng shui con un significado en cada curva, ángulo y perspectiva. Las habitaciones están concebidas para abrazar las puestas de sol y los ocasos en relación con los cumpleaños y aniversarios familiares. Acero y cristal crean ondas y curvas, la piedra flota y la madera en tonos poco habituales resulta natural. Una multitud de colores y superficies pintadas a mano expresan el peculiar carácter de esta residencia llena de energía.

First Floor

Second Floor

Hammonds Residence

HOUSE + HOUSE ARCHITECTS
house@ix.netcom.com

This 2,800 square-foot home was a replacement for one of the many houses destroyed in Oakland's tragic firestorm. To take advantage of the steeply sloping terrain, the house was lowered to make space for broad decks and private gardens. Three distinct volumes are linked by a dramatic 40-foot stairway and a large central terrace. A vaulted steel canopy provides an entrance down to the main living spaces. A cylindrical dining room links the volumes and a curved deck further reinforces the circular theme. The wide-ranging materials, including steel, concrete, oak, cherry, limestone, granite, stucco and cedar, are used in complimentary combinations, and each has been given a different finish to create a specific effect.

Dieses 260 m² große Haus entstand an der Stelle eines bei der Feuersbrunst von Oakland zerstörten Gebäudes. Um das abschüssige Grundstück sinnvoll auszunutzen, wurde das Haus niedriger gebaut und Raum für weitläufige Terrassen und Gärten geschaffen. Eine eindrucksvolle 12 m lange Treppe und eine große Terrasse verbinden drei Baukörper. Ein gewölbtes Stahlvordach geleitet ins Innere und hinab in die Hauptwohnräume. Das zylindrische Esszimmer erschließt die Räume und eine geschwungene Terrasse akzentuiert die Kreisthematik. Die ausgewählten Materialien – darunter Stahl, Beton, Eiche, Kirschbaum, Kalkstein, Granit, Stuck und Zeder – sind effektvoll in gefälligen Kombinationen und unterschiedlichen Ausführungen eingesetzt.

Completion date: **1998**

Cette maison de 260 m² remplace un demeure détruite par l'incendie tragique d'Oakland. Tirant parti du site en pente, la maison a été abaissée et ouvre la voie à de larges terrasses et jardins privatifs. Trois volumes distincts sont reliés par un spectaculaire escalier de 12 m et une vaste terrasse centrale. Un auvent voûté en acier mène à l'intérieur et vers les espaces de vie principaux. La salle à manger cylindrique relie les volumes et une terrasse courbe renforce le thème circulaire. La palette des matériaux a combiné l'acier, le béton, le chêne, le cerisier, le combe, le granite, le stuc et le cèdre pour offrir des finitions diverses et créer un effet spécifique.

Esta casa de 260 m² reemplaza otra destruida en el incendio de Oakland. Para aprovechar su situación escalonada, se bajó la altura de la casa que ahora se abre a las amplias cubiertas y jardines privados. Tres volúmenes distintos se comunican por una teatral escalera de 12 m y una gran terraza central. Un toldo de acero abovedado conduce al interior y a los espacios de vivienda del piso de abajo. Un comedor cilíndrico une los volúmenes, y una cubierta curva se encarga de reforzar este carácter circular. La paleta de materiales –acero, hormigón, roble, cerezo, piedra caliza, granito, estuco y cedro– se usó en combinaciones complementarias con acabados diferentes para dotar a cada una de un efecto específico.

First Floor

Second Floor

Schein Residence

HOUSE + HOUSE ARCHITECTS

house@ix.netcom.com

Perched on the northern crest of a hill overlooking the bay, this renovation and extension transformed a 1950s ranch house into a dramatic space layered with bold colors and contrasting materials. The new integrated living and dining room is divided into areas by sculpted elements, like the deep melon-colored fireplace and the maple walls gridded with aluminum channels, and the variations in ceiling materials and colors. The new deck off the family room has stainless steel cable railings with redwood posts and top. Oak flooring, maple cabinets, stainless-steel appliances, African slate, black mosaic and deep, intense colors define the character of this residence in Tiburon, San Francisco.

Durch Aus- und Umbau wurde dieses auf dem Nordkamm eines die Bucht überblickenden Hügels gelegene Ranchhaus der 1950er Jahren in einen lebendigen, von kühnen Farben und kontrastierenden Materialien gefassten Raum verwandelt. Das neue Wohn-/Esszimmer wird durch skulpturale Elemente wie den Kamin im Ton dunkler Melone oder die von einem Netz aus Aluminiumschienen durchzogenen Ahornwände sowie durch wechselnde Deckenmaterialien und -farben untergliedert. Die neue Dachterrasse hat Edelstahlseilgeländer mit Pfosten und Überdachung aus Rotholz. Eichenfußböden, Ahornschränke, Edelstahlgeräte, afrikanischer Schiefer, schwarzes Mosaik und dunkle, intensive Farben prägen dieses Wohnhaus in Tiburon, San Francisco.

Completion date: **2002**

Sur la crête Nord d'une colline
dominant la baie, cette rénovation a
transformé un ranch années 1950 en
un espace spectaculaire aux couleurs
vives et aux matériaux contrastés.
Séjour et salle à manger, réunis, sont
divisés par des éléments sculptés : la
cheminée couleur melon sombre, les
murs d'érable parcourus d'aluminium
et les plafonds aux matériaux et
couleurs changeants. La terrasse de la
chambre familiale compte une
balustrade câblée d'acier et des
montants et un toit en séquoia.
Parquet de chêne, placards en érable,
décorations en inox, ardoises
africaines, mosaïque noire et couleurs
profondes et intenses définissent cette
résidence de Tiburon à San Francisco.

Situada en la cima de una colina que
domina la bahía, esta casa rancho de
los años 1950 fue transformada en un
teatral escenario de colores audaces y
materiales contrastados. El nuevo
espacio integrado de salón comedor
muestra áreas diferenciadas por
elementos esculturales como una
profunda chimenea color melón,
paredes de arce con acanalados de
aluminio y fuertes contrastes en los
materiales y colores del techo. La
nueva cubierta de la sala familiar tiene
barandillas de acero inoxidable con
postes y molduras y un tejadillo de
madera roja. Parquet de roble,
armarios de arce, electrodomésticos de
acero inoxidable, pizarra africana,
mosaicos negros y colores profundos e
intensos definen el carácter de esta
residencia de Tiburón, San Francisco.

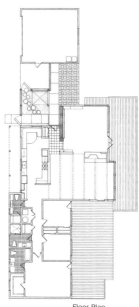

Floor Plan

Telegraph Hill Residence

HOUSE + HOUSE ARCHITECTS
house@ix.netcom.com

A small 1906 earthquake-relief home, which has accumulated additions over the decades, marks the site for this refurbished residence, located in the center of a block and surrounded by the gardens of its neighbors. Directly behind the home stands one of the largest Japanese maple trees in Northern California, and this became the focal point around which the new home evolved. Under the shadow of the city's historic Coit Tower, the house still appears to be a tiny wood-sided bungalow from the street. Inside, however, an 18-foot-high grid of windows overlooking the maple tree creates a powerful first impression. Colored concrete, perforated steel and geometric fittings all give rise to a unique and dynamic residence.

Ein kleines, im Laufe der Jahrzehnte ausgebautes Ausweichquartier des Erdbebens von 1906 bildete den Ausgangspunkt für dieses umgebaute Haus, das umgeben von den Gärten der Nachbarn in der Mitte eines Blocks liegt. Direkt hinter dem Haus steht einer der größten japanischen Ahornbäume Nordkaliforniens, Mittelpunkt der Entwicklung des neuen Hauses. Das im Schatten des historischen Coit Tower gelegene Haus ist von der Straße her noch immer ein kleiner Holzbungalow. Im Inneren jedoch beeindruckt ein 5,5 m hohes, Sprossenfenster, das den Ahorn einfasst. Farbiger Beton, perforierter Stahl und geometrische Ausstattungselemente schaffen ein einzigartiges und dynamisches Wohnhaus.

Completion date: **1996**

Une petite maison du séisme de 1906, produit d'ajouts au cours du temps, marque le site de cette résidence rénovée, au centre d'un bloc et des jardins avoisinants. Directement derrière la demeure se trouve l'un des plus grands érables japonais de Californie du nord, devenu le point focal autour duquel la maison gravite. À l'ombre de l'historique Coit Tower, la demeure n'est toujours qu'un petit bungalow à deux pas de la rue. À l'intérieur, pourtant, un patchwork vitré de 5,5 m embrassant l'érable japonais offre une saisissante première impression. Béton coloré, acier perforé et éclairages géométriques génèrent une résidence unique et dynamique.

Esta residencia situada en el centro de un bloque entre los jardines de las casas vecinas fue en su origen un pequeño refugio construido a raíz del terremoto de 1906. Justo detrás del edificio se alza uno de los arces japoneses más viejos de California Norte. Por ello, la nueva construcción se desarrolló alrededor del árbol. A la sombra de la histórica Coit Tower, la casa parece desde la calle un minúsculo bungalow de madera. Por el contrario, en el interior, un juego de ventanas de 5,5 m de altura desde las que se comtempla el arce, causa una gran impresión. Hormigón pintado, acero perforado e instalaciones geométricas generan una vivienda de carácter único y dinámico.

First Floor

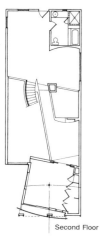

Second Floor

Airaghi Residence

A+D ARCHITECTURE
info@a-plus-d.com

This project reinterprets urban family living within a conventional two-story Edwardian house by introducing an open-plan living scheme. The new space is shared by a kitchen, dining-room and lounge on the lower level, with tall windows and skylights so that sunlight stretches across the elongated room. A wooden staircase with a series of closets leads up to the new floor with sleeping quarters, crowned by a glass skylight. The thoughtful fusion of old and new informs the design. The elevated ground floor deck extends the social space outdoors, while the bedroom and bathroom upstairs open onto the terrace, with its spectacular views of the city.

Bei diesem Projekt wird städtisches Familienleben in einem zweigeschossigen eduardianischen Standardhaus durch die Einführung eines offenen Wohnmodells neu interpretiert. Den unteren Raum mit hohen Fenstern und Dachfenstern teilen sich Küche, Esszimmer und Wohnbereich, sodass das Licht durch den lang gestreckten Raum fließt. Eine Holztreppe mit Schränken stellt die Verbindung zu einer neuen Etage mit Schlafzimmern her, die von einem Oberlicht gekrönt wird. Das wohl bedachte Aufeinandertreffen von Alt und Neu prägt das Design. Die erhöhte Terrasse im Erdgeschoss verlängert den Gemeinschaftsraum ins Freie, während oben Schlafzimmer und Bad auf die Terrasse mit einer spektakulären Sicht auf die Stadt führen.

Completion date: **2000**

Ce projet réinterprète la vie de la famille urbaine dans une maison edwardienne de deux niveaux en introduisant un plan ouvert. Le nouvel espace est partagé par des aires cuisine, repas, famille et séjour au premier niveau, les grandes fenêtres et claires-voies diffusant dans la longue pièce. Un escalier de bois incorporant une série de placards connecte le nouvel étage, le coin dortoir, couronné d'une claire-voie de verre. L'alliance avisée ancien/nouveau guide le design. Le palier du bas, en élévation, prolonge les espaces communs à l'extérieur alors que la chambre et le bain, en haut, s'ouvrent sur une terrasse aux vues spectaculaires sur la cité.

Este proyecto reinterpreta la vida de una familia urbana en una tradicional casa eduardiana de dos pisos introduciendo un concepto de vivienda abierta. El nuevo espacio de la planta baja acoge la cocina, el comedor y un salón de altas ventanas y tragaluces para que penetre la luz. Una escalera de madera con armarios incorporados conduce a la nueva planta de los dormitorios, coronada por una claraboya de cristal. La cuidada mezcla de elementos antiguos y modernos define el diseño. La cubierta elevada de la planta baja extiende los espacios sociales hacia el exterior, mientras que el dormitorio y el baño del piso de arriba se abren a una terraza con espectaculares vistas sobre la ciudad.

Floor Plan

Elevations

A + D ARCHITECTURE
info@a-plus-d.com

An "earthquake shack", a small, temporary, mass-produced wooden dwelling made to accommodate victims of the 1906 earthquake, was turned into a loft by modernizing its facilities and creating an open living space. The original house was transported to its present location in 1920 and placed on top of a basement. The architects took on the challenge of reinterpreting this model, raising the structure by one and a half stories and converting it into two residential apartments. The original wooden floors have been retained, while stacked double-height spaces have been connected to the old shack by a gallery that serves as a bridge between the old and the new.

Eine „Erdbebenbaracke", eine kleine provisorische Holzbehausung, in Serie zur Unterbringung der Erdbebenopfer von 1906 hergestellt, wurde modernisiert und zum Loft geöffnet. Die ursprüngliche Unterkunft wurde 1920 an ihren gegenwärtigen Standort geschafft und auf ein Fundament gesetzt. Die Architekten stellten sich der Herausforderung einer Neuinterpretation dieses Modells und erhöhten das Tragwerk um eineinhalb Stockwerke, um so zwei Wohnungen entstehen zu lassen. Zwei übereinander liegende Räume von doppelter Höhe wurden mit der ursprünglichen Unterkunft verbunden und die Originalholzböden erhalten, wobei eine als Brücke zwischen Alt und Neu fungierende Galerie hinzugefügt wurde.

Completion date: **2001**

Un « abri sismique », une petit refuge en bois fabriqué en série pour accueillir les victimes du séisme de 1906, est devenu un loft en transformant ses systèmes et en insérant une possibilité de séjour ouvert. La demeure originale a été amenée sur le site actuel et placée sur des fondations 1920. Les architectes ont relevé le défi de la réinterprétation du modèle, relevant la structure d'un niveau et demi pour la convertir en deux logements résidentiels. Deux espaces à double hauteur sont connectés à la maison d'origine et les sols sont préservés, incorporant une galerie servant de pont entre l'ancien et le nouveau.

Una "cabaña de terremoto", un refugio provisional de madera construido en serie para dar cobijo a las víctimas del terremoto de 1906, fue transformado en un loft, actualizando la infraestructura y convirtiéndolo en una vivienda abierta. La casita original se trasladó y se cimentó en su localización actual en 1920. Los arquitectos se enfrentaron al reto de reinterpretar el modelo levantando la estructura en un piso y medio para convertirla así en dos apartamentos. Dos espacios verticales de doble altura comunican con el refugio original. Se conservaron los suelos de madera antiguos, y se incorporó una galería que sirve de puente entre la parte nueva y la vieja.

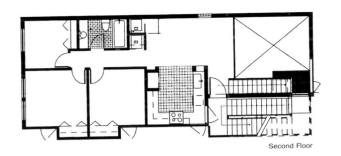

Second Floor

Corson
Residence

LEDDY MAYTUM STACEY ARCHITECTS
rsheinberg@lmsarch.com

This graphic design/photography studio and residence is located on a small, narrow lot in San Francisco's South of Market district. The project developed as a response to a modest budget and a rigorous esthetic sensibility. High spaces are enclosed with inexpensive, maintenance-free industrial materials, some of which are meticulously finished while others were deliberately left exposed to preserve and emphasize the industrial feel. Worn floors and old wood furniture mingle with polished wood and stainless-steel surfaces. An interesting collection of artwork and furniture complements the diversity expressed by the varied yet disciplined use of materials and colors.

Dieses Grafikdesign-/Fotoatelier und Wohnhaus liegt auf einem kleinen, schmalen Grundstück im South-of-Market-Viertel. Das Projekt antwortet auf ein bescheidenes Budget und eine ausgeprägte ästhetische Sensibilität. Hohe Räume wurden in preiswerte, pflegeleichte Industriematerialien gekleidet, von denen einige sorgfältig bearbeitet wurden, während andere absichtsvoll offen liegen, um den industriellen Eindruck zu bewahren und hervorzuheben. Böden mit Patina und alte Holzmöbel harmonieren mit Oberflächen aus poliertem Holz und Edelstahl. Eine interessante Kunst- und Möbelauswahl vervollständigt die durch den abwechslungsreichen und doch disziplinierten Gebrauch von Materialien und Farbtönen ausgedrückte Vielfalt.

Completion date: **1991**

Cet atelier de design/photo et résidence se situe sur une petite parcelle étroite du district de South of Market. Le projet est une réponse à un budget modeste et une sensibilité esthétique rigoriste. De hauts volumes sont ceints de matériaux industriels peu coûteux et sans entretien, dont certains décorés avec soin et d'autres volontairement à nu pour préserver et souligner le caractère industriel. Les sols usés et le vieux mobilier en bois jouent avec le bois lustré et les surfaces d'acier inox. Une intéressante collection artistique et de pièces de mobilier complète la diversité exprimée l'usage varié mais discipliné des tons et matériaux.

Este estudio de fotografía y diseño gráfico y residencia está en un pequeño y estrecho solar del distrito de South of Market. El proyecto responde a una rigurosa sensibilidad estética con un modesto presupuesto. Los altos espacios vienen definidos por materiales industriales económicos que no exigen mantenimiento, algunos acabados con mucho detalle y, otros, deliberadamente explícitos para preservar y enfatizar el aire industrial. Suelos gastados y muebles de vieja madera se entremezclan con superficies de madera pulida y acero inoxidable. Una interesante colección de arte y mobiliario complementa la diversidad expresada por un uso de materiales y tonos variado, pero disciplinado.

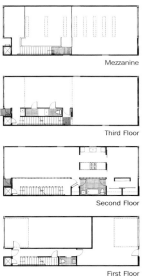

Mezzanine

Third Floor

Second Floor

First Floor

273

WILLIAM LEDDY/LEDDY MAYTUM STACEY ARCHITECTS
rsheinberg@lmsarch.com

This studio and residence was inserted into an existing building in a dense, semi-industrial area of San Francisco. To compensate for the constricted site, the primary aim of the project was to introduce as much light as possible into the living spaces. This was achieved in a number of ways: a glassed inner courtyard, slots between walls and skylights. The interior spaces are organized around a path integral to the building and used to move large canvases. Both the living and working spaces are characterized by surfaces in subdued tones and colorful objects, which combine to create a casual and light-hearted atmosphere.

Diese Atelierwohnung wurde in einem bestehenden Gebäude in einem dicht bebauten und halb industriellen Viertel eingerichtet. Aufgrund der räumlichen Enge bestand das Hauptziel darin, so viel Licht wie nur möglich in die Wohnräume hereinzulassen. Dies geschah auf verschiedenerlei Art: durch einen verglasten Innenhof und Schlitze zwischen den Wänden und Dachfenster. Die Anlage der inneren Räume folgte einer Linie, die von dem für den Transport großer Leinwände bestimmten Gebäude vorgegeben wurde. Die Wohn- und Arbeitsbereiche werden durch eine Kombination heller Oberflächen und farbenfroher Gegenstände geprägt, wodurch eine lockere und unbeschwerte Atmosphäre erzeugt wird.

Completion date: **1988**

Cet atelier-résidence a été inséré dans un édifice existant situé dans une zone dense et toujours semi industrielle de San Francisco. Les contraintes du site ont donné comme objectif premier au projet d'introduire le plus de lumière possible dans les espaces de vie, et de plusieurs façons : une cour intérieur vitrée et des fentes dans les murs et des claires-voies. L'espace intérieur est organisé autour d'un chemin offert par l'édifice, prévu pour transporter de grandes toiles. Les lieux de vie et de travail sont caractérisés par une combinaison de surfaces claires et d'objets colorés créant une ambiance détendue et gaie.

Este estudio vivienda se construyó en el interior de un edificio situado en un área densamente habitada con cierta actividad industrial. A causa del asfixiante entorno, el primer objetivo del proyecto fue permitir la entrada del máximo de luz posible en las áreas de vivienda, lo que se consiguió gracias a diferentes recursos como un patio interior acristalado, aberturas entre paredes y claraboyas. Los espacios interiores están organizados alrededor de un corredor del edificio pensado para el transporte de grandes lienzos. Ambos espacios, de trabajo y vivienda, están caracterizados por una combinación de superficies luminosas y objetos de gran colorido que crean una atmósfera casual y diáfana.

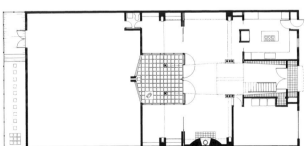

Floor Plan

Martin III

WILLIAM LEDDY/LEDDY MAYTUM STACEY ARCHITECTS
rsheinberg@lmsarch.com

This house is located on Telegraph Hill, with some of the best views of both the city and bay. The terrain and the house are organized in the form of narrow parallel bands. The building is exposed on four sides, with light entering in a variety of ways throughout the year, running along tall walls, pouring down the central stairway and filtering through the overhead skylights. Tall aluminum and glass sliding doors at either end of the house provide unimpeded views as well as plenty of cross ventilation. The interiors feature pale colors and a sober design. The exterior materials were obviously selected with the weather conditions in mind, but they also accentuate the formal organization.

Das Haus liegt auf dem Telegraph Hill mit einer der besten Aussichten auf Stadt und Bucht. Grundstück und Haus bilden schmale parallele Bänder. Da es nach allen vier Seiten frei steht, dringt Licht das ganze Jahr über auf vielerlei Art in das Gebäude ein: es streift über hohe Wände, zieht sich die zentrale Treppe hinunter und sickert von oben durch Dachfenster. Hohe Schiebetüren aus Glas und Aluminium an den Enden des Hauses sorgen für eine uneingeschränkte Sicht und eine hervorragende Durchlüftung. Das Interieur ist geprägt von hellen Tönen und einem nüchternen Design. Die Außenmaterialien wurden offensichtlich entsprechend der klimatischen Verhältnisse ausgewählt, unterstreichen jedoch zugleich die Formensprache.

Completion date: **2001**

Cette maison sur Telegraph Hill jouit de certaines des plus belles vues sur la ville et la baie. Le site et la demeure s'organisent en fines tranches d'espace parallèles Exposée des quatre côtés, la lumière s'invite de diverses façons durant l'année, balayant les hauts murs, se projetant sur l'escalier central et filtrant par les claires-voies. De hautes portes coulissantes en aluminium aux extrémités optimisent l'accès aux vues ainsi qu'à une aération abondante. L'intérieur, au design sobre, s'affiche en des tons légers. Les matériaux extérieurs ont été choisis pour vieillir naturellement et accentuer l'organisation formelle.

Esta casa, ubicada en la cumbre de Telegraph Hill, disfruta de espléndidas vistas sobre la ciudad y la bahía. Solar y edificio están organizados en estrechas franjas de espacios paralelos. La luz que entra por los cuatro costados de forma diferente según la estación del año baña las altas paredes, proyecta la sombra de la escalera central y se filtra por las claraboyas superiores. Esbeltas puertas corredizas de aluminio y cristal a ambos lados de la casa proporcionan un máximo acceso a las vistas y muy buena ventilación. El interior ofrece tonos luminosos y un diseño sobrio. Para el exterior se seleccionaron materiales que envejecen de forma natural y acentúan la organización formal.

Third Floor

Second Floor

First Floor

Garage

85 Natoma

JIM JENNINGS
jjennings@jimjenningsarchitecture.com

This residential/workplace loft building was primarily commissioned as a design project to exhibit the esthetic potential of new contemporary constructions in the city. The intention of both client and architect was to create a unique yet understated profile that would liven up the neighborhood with its distinctive but simple design. This concept resulted in a vaulted building with no transition between the wall and the roof. The visual smoothness of the curved steel subverts the common perception that is a hard metal, while the generous use of glass provides a dramatic relationship between the interior spaces and the surrounding urban landscape. The double-height volumes maximise energy conservation through their concrete floors and radiating heat.

Dieses Gebäude mit Lofts zum Wohnen und Arbeiten entstand vorrangig als Designprojekt, um das ästhetische Potenzial neuer zeitgenössischer Bauten zu zeigen. Auftraggeber wie Architekt wünschten ein besonderes und gleichzeitig unaufdringliches Profil, das den Bestand mit seinem trotz allem schlichten Design beleben sollte. So entstand ein Gebäude mit gewölbten Formen, ohne Übergang zwischen Mauer und Dach. Die optische Geschmeidigkeit des gebogenen Stahls widerspricht dem typischen Eindruck von hartem Metall, während der großzügige Einsatz von Glas Spannung zwischen dem Innenraum und der Umgebung erzeugt. Die Baukörper von doppelter Höhe optimieren die Energieeinsparung durch Betonböden und der Strahlungswärme.

Completion date: **2002**

L'immeuble de lofts séjour/travail était essentiellement un projet de design pour présenter le potentiel esthétique des nouveaux édifices contemporains dans la ville. Client et architecte avait pour intention de créer un profil unique mais sobre animant les alentours grâce à une conception distincte mais simple. Ce concept se traduit par un bâtiment en voûte sans transition du mur au toit. Le lissé visuel de l'acier courbe contredit la perception traditionnellement dure du métal, alors que l'usage généreux du verre apporte une relation spectaculaire entre les espaces intérieurs et le tissu urbain environnant. Les volumes à double hauteur maximisent la conservation d'énergie grâce aux sols en béton et à la chaleur radiante.

Este edificio de lofts destinados a vivienda y lugar de trabajo fue encargado como un proyecto para exhibir el potencial estético de las nuevas construcciones contemporáneas en la ciudad. La intención del cliente y del arquitecto era lograr un perfil único y hasta ahora subestimado que animase el barrio con un diseño diferente pero simple. El concepto se convirtió en un edificio de formas abovedadas sin transición entre paredes y techo. La suavidad visual del acero curvado contradice la natural dureza del metal, mientras que el generoso uso del cristal crea una dramática relación entre los espacios interiores y la fábrica urbana que los acoge. Los volúmenes de doble altura maximizan el ahorro de energía con sus suelos de hormigón con calefacción radiante.

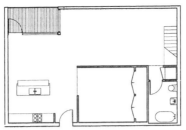

Floor Plan

304 **Oliver Residence**

JIM JENNINGS
jjennings@jimjenningsarchitecture.com

A procession of perimeter glass walls, reflecting pools and landscaped gardens leads to this impressive home situated on Telegraph Hill, in the shadow of the city's landmark, Coit Tower. The clients, avid art collectors, wanted not only comfortable living spaces but also galleries to display their collection, an apartment for visiting artists, and an extra bedroom for family visitors. The architect spread these requirements over four levels, unified internally by a large concrete cylinder that culminates in a large roof terrace made entirely of glass. Jennings displays a skilful and graceful handling of verticality to imbue the space with light, warmth and a dramatic view of the city skyline.

Verschiedene Verglasungen, spiegelnde Pools und angelegte Gärten führen zu diesem beeindruckenden Haus auf dem Telegraph Hill im Schatten des Coit Tower, dem Wahrzeichen der Stadt. Die Auftraggeber, eifrige Kunstsammler, wünschten sich komfortable Wohnräume, Galerien zum Ausstellen ihrer Sammlung, ein Gästeapartment für Künstler und ein zusätzliches Schlafzimmer für Verwandtenbesuche. Der Architekt streckte das Programm über vier Etagen, die durch einen großen Betonzylinder vereint werden, der in eine große, ganz aus Glas gestaltete Dachterrasse mündet. Jennings gestaltet geschickt und anmutig die Vertikalität, um den Raum mit Licht, Wärme und einem eindrucksvollen Blick auf die Skyline zu durchtränken.

Completion date: **2002**

Un premier plan processionnel de murs d'enceinte en verre, de piscines réfléchissantes et de jardins paysagers mène à cette demeure saisissante de Telegraph Hill, à l'ombre de la célèbre Coit Tower. Collectionneurs d'art, les clients souhaitaient des espaces de vie confortables, des galeries pour leur collection, un appartement pour les artistes invités et une chambre pour les visites familiales. L'architecte a organisé le programme sur quatre niveaux unifiés par un grand cylindre de béton culminant sur un toit en terrasse entièrement vitré. Jennings traite la verticalité avec art et grâce pour imprégner l'espace de lumière, de chaleur et de vues spectaculaires sur la ville.

Un entorno de paredes de cristal, piscinas que reflejan la luz del sol y cuidados jardines conducen a esta impresionante casa situada en Telegraph Hill, a la sombra de la emblemática Coit Tower. El cliente, un apasionado coleccionista de arte, quería estancias confortables, galerías para exponer su colección, un apartamento para huéspedes artistas y un dormitorio adicional para las visitas de la familia. El arquitecto organizó el programa sobre cuatro niveles unificados en el interior por un gran cilindro de hormigón que culmina en una amplia azotea totalmente hecha de cristal. Jenning hace un hábil y elegante uso de la verticalidad para dar al espacio luz, calidez y una espléndida vista de la ciudad.

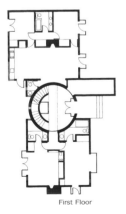

First Floor

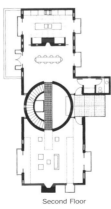

Second Floor

Third Floor

Astrolab House

HEYDAR GHIAÏ & SONS, INC.
architect@ghiai.com

Yves Ghiaï, son of Heydar Ghiaï, known as the father of modern Iranian architecture, designed this house on one of the city's highest hills, with panoramic views of the bay. The entire building was built in reinforced concrete and it consists of a broken ellipsoid staircase with no support between the floors. Inspired by ancient Persian navigational devices and astronomical instruments, most particularly the astrolabe, a wealth of curves express planetary rotation, skylights frame the moonlight and the facades contain elements symbolizing the sun and the moon. The flowing interior spaces reflect the transcendental aspect of Persian mystical culture, which has had such a profound influence on the architect.

Yves Ghiaï, der Sohn des als Vater der modernen iranischen Architektur bekannten Heydar Ghiaï, entwarf dieses auf einem der höchsten Hügel der Stadt gelegene Haus mit Panoramasicht über die Bucht. Das gesamte Gebäude besteht aus Stahlbeton und wird von einer unterbrochenen ellipsenförmigen, frei tragenden Treppe bestimmt. Inspiriert von antiken persischen Navigationsgeräten und astronomischen Instrumenten, insbesondere vom Astrolabium, drücken zahlreiche Wölbungen planetare Bewegungen aus, rahmen Dachluken das Mondlicht ein und Fassadenelemente symbolisieren Sonne und Mond. Die fließenden Innenräume spiegeln den fundamentalen Aspekt der persischen Mystik wider, die den Architekt stark beeinflusst hat.

Completion date: **1996**

Yves Ghiaï, fils d'Heydar Ghiaï, père de l'architecture moderne en Iran, a conçu cette maison aux vues panoramiques sur la baie, située sur l'une des plus hautes collines de la cité. L'ensemble de l'édifice est en béton renforcé et consiste en un escalier ellipsoïde brisé, sans soutien entre les étages. Inspirées d'instruments astronomiques et de navigation perses, surtout l'astrolabe, des courbes multiples expriment la rotation planétaire, des claires-voies encadrent le clair de lune et les façades arborent des éléments symbolisant soleil et lune. La fluidité intérieure reflète la transcendence de la mystique culture perse, une influence profonde de l'architecte.

Yves Ghiaï, hijo de Heydar Ghiaï y conocedor como su padre de la arquitectura iraní moderna, diseñó esta casa sobre una de las colinas más altas de la ciudad, con vistas panorámicas sobre la bahía. Todo el edificio se construyó con hormigón reforzado en torno a una escalera elipsoidal partida sin soportes entre pisos. Inspirada en los antiguos instrumentos de astronomía y navegación persas, particularmente en el astrolabio, una multitud de líneas curvas expresa la rotación planetaria, varias claraboyas enmarcan la luz de la luna y las fachadas contienen elementos de simbolismo solar y lunar. Los fluidos espacios interiores reflejan el aspecto más trascendental de la cultura mística persa que tanto le ha influido al arquitecto.

Residence Royale

HEYDAR GHIAÏ & SONS
architect@ghiai.com

A less recent project by the legendary Iranian architects settled in San Francisco, this residence is one of three luxury homes in the five-floor condominium. The building was built entirely out of steel and concrete and an innovative floating foundation system patented by the architect was used to prevent seismic disruptions. Once again influenced by Persian mysticism, the facade incorporates an inverted parabola to collect cosmic energy, while the vertical steps symbolize the distribution of that energy into each living unit. The street facade is primarily made up of right angles, symbolizing a structured society, while the rounded and curvilinear glass walls overlooking the garden represent the more human aspect of the living spaces.

Diese Wohnung, ein älteres Projekt der in San Francisco lebenden legendären iranischen Architekten, ist eines von drei Luxusappartements in einem fünfgeschossigen Haus. Im Gebäude aus Stahl und Beton wurde ein innovatives, vom Architekten patentiertes System schwimmender Fundamente gegen erdbebenbedingte Risse eingebaut. Die von persischer Mystik beeinflusste Fassade zeigt eine umgekehrte Parabel zum Einfangen kosmischer Energie, während die vertikalen Stufen die Verteilung dieser Energie in die Wohnbereiche symbolisieren. Zur Straßen herrschen rechte Winkel als Symbol der gesellschaftlichen Struktur vor, während die abgerundeten Glaswände zum Garten den menschlicheren Aspekt der Wohnräume darstellen.

Completion date: **1992**

Projet moins récent des légendaires architectes iraniens de San Francisco, cette résidence est l'un des trois logements de luxe d'une copropriété de cinq étages. L'édifice, intégralement en acier et en béton, compte un système novateur de fondations flottantes antisismique, breveté par l'architecte. À nouveau sous influence du mysticisme perse, la façade affiche une parabole inversée recueillant l'énergie cosmique, ses échelons verticaux en symbolisant la distribution dans chaque lieu de vie. La façade sur rue comprend essentiellement des angles droits, symboles d'une société structurée, et celle du jardin aux parois vitrées et curvilignes représente l'aspect humain des espaces de séjour.

Esta residencia, un proyecto no tan reciente de los legendarios arquitectos iraníes establecidos en San Francisco, es una de las tres lujosas viviendas de un condominio de cinco pisos. El edificio, de acero y hormigón, incorpora un sistema de cimientos flotantes resistentes a los seísmos patentado por el propio arquitecto. Influencia una vez más del misticismo persa, la fachada incorpora una parábola invertida para recoger la energía cósmica, y las escalinatas verticales representan la distribución de esa energía en cada unidad de la vivienda. La fachada que da a la calle muestra básicamente ángulos rectos que simbolizan la sociedad estructurada, mientras que la del jardín, de paredes de cristal curvilíneas, representa el carácter más humano del interior.

Belvedere Residence

CASS CALDER SMITH
cass@ccs.architecture.com

Designed as the main home for a family of five, this project is a complete renovation of a two-story residence located right next to the bay, in between the street and the water.
An axis leads to the house, pierces through the two-story central hall and continues to the bay as a dock. This axial organization revolves round the central hall, flanked by the living-dining area on one side and the kitchen and family room on the other. Both sections have identical openings, setting up connections with the landscape and water. The interior is a restrained palette of white walls, limestone floors, natural wood and steel.

Für eine fünfköpfige Familie wurde ein zweigeschossiges Wohnhaus, das direkt an der Bucht zwischen Straße und Wasser liegt, komplett renoviert. Eine Achse führt durch das Haus, durchquert die sich über zwei Etagen erstreckende Eingangshalle und setzt sich zur Bucht als Anleger fort. Diese Organisation entlang einer Achse zieht sich durch die zentrale Eingangshalle, die Wohn- und Essbereich auf der einen Seite sowie Küche und zweites Wohnzimmer auf der anderen flankieren. Beide Bereiche sind in gleicher Weise geöffnet, wodurch eine Verbindung zu Landschaft und Wasser hergestellt wird. Das Interieur verwendet eine maßvolle Farbskala mit weißen Wänden, Kalksteinböden, naturbelassenem Holz und Stahl.

Completion date: **1997**

Foyer principal d'une famille de cinq personnes, ce projet est une rénovation complète d'une maison de deux étages située le long de la baie, entre la rue et la mer. Un axe mène à la demeure, transperce le hall central de deux niveaux pour devenir un ponton sur la baie. Cette organisation axiale passe par un hall flanqué des zones de séjour et de repas d'un côté et de la cuisine et de la pièce familiale de l'autre. Les deux zones disposent d'ouvertures les connectant au paysage et à la mer. L'intérieur respecte une palette restreinte de murs blancs, de sols en combe, de bois naturel et d'acier.

Planeada como la primera residencia de una familia de cinco miembros, este proyecto es una reforma completa de una casa de dos pisos situada cerca de la bahía, entre la calle y el agua. Un eje conduce a la casa, atraviesa el hall central de dos pisos y continúa hasta la bahía como un muelle. Esta organización del eje en transversal se extiende a lo largo del hall central flanqueado por el área de salón comedor a un lado y la cocina y otro salón por el otro. Ambas áreas poseen aperturas similares que las comunican con el paisaje y el agua. El discreto interior está determinado por paredes blancas, suelos de piedra caliza, madera natural y acero.

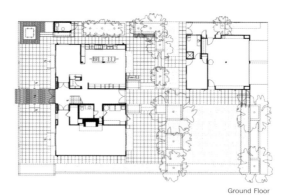

Ground Floor

Cole Valley Residence

CASS CALDER SMITH
cass@ccs.architecture.com

This project in Cole Valley involved the addition of a third-floor master bedroom, bathroom and roof deck on an existing two-story residence, to take advantage the 180-degree views of the San Francisco Bay. A gently curved roof organizes the top-floor extension. The ceiling is lined with natural cedar planks, while the cut-limestone bathroom complements the pale tones and clean lines of the flush trimless windows. The living room on the second floor features a staircase with solid maple treads and open risers, set off by a shiny, backlit acrylic guardrail, and, on the opposite wall, a series of built-in cherry-wood shelves, a skylight and a concrete fireplace.

Auf das vorhandene zweigeschossige Wohnhaus in Cole Valley wurde eine dritte Etage mit großem Schlafzimmer, Bad und Dachterrasse aufgestockt, um die Rundumsicht auf die Bucht genießen zu können. Ein sanft gewölbtes Dach ist das bestimmende Element. Die Decke ist mit Planken aus naturbelassener Zeder gestaltet, während der behauene Kalkstein des Bades mit den hellen Tönen und klaren Linien der glatten, rahmenlosen Fenster harmoniert. Im Wohnzimmer im zweiten Stock fällt eine Treppe aus massivem Ahorn ohne Setzstufen ins Auge, die durch ein schimmerndes, von hinten beleuchtetes Acrylgeländer abgesetzt wird, sowie Einbauregale in Kirschbaum an der gegenüberliegenden Wand, ein Dachfenster und ein Betonkamin.

Completion date: **2002**

Ce projet de Cole Valley a impliqué l'ajout d'un troisième étage incluant chambre principale, bain et terrasse a une résidence de deux niveaux pour tirer parti des vues à 180 degrés sur la baie. Un toit doucement courbé organise le nouvel étage. Ses plafonds sont couverts de cèdre naturel alors le bain en combe taillée complète les tons clairs et les lignes nettes des fenêtres dépouillées. Le séjour du second propose un escalier en érable massif et ajouré délimité par une balustrade acrylique rétro-éclairée et, sur le mur opposé, une série d'étagères intégrées en cerisier, une claire-voie et une cheminée en béton.

Este proyecto en Cole Valley añadió un tercer nivel con un dormitorio, un baño y una azotea a una casa de dos plantas para aprovechar la vista de 180 grados sobre la bahía. Un tejado de curvas pronunciadas delimita el piso superior. El techo está cruzado por paneles de cedro natural, mientras que el baño con piedra caliza tallada complementa los tonos luminosos y las claras líneas de las ventanas empotradas sin ornamentos. El salón de la segunda planta luce una escalera de sólidos peldaños de arce sin contrahuellas contenida por una barandilla acrílica iluminada desde atrás y, en la pared opuesta, una serie de estanterías empotradas de cerezo, una claraboya y una chimenea de hormigón.

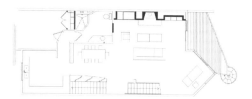

Second Floor

Third Floor

House in
Marin County

JANET CORAL CAMPBELL
campbellarchitec@aol.com

An existing property was renovated and designed to take in light and to embrace the views of the Bay. The redwood grove on one side was preserved, with a walkway hacked out to lead to the front door and multi-level decks. This owner asked for a minimalist design, as well as nautical features along the exterior decks, a wide, open fireplace and an open-plan kitchen on the main level. Skylights were put in wherever possible, for example in the large quadrangle in the center of the kitchen and living area. The master bedroom is situated on the quieter end of the main level and has access to two decks, an en-suite bathroom and a closet with a skylight.

Ein bestehendes Anwesen wurde renoviert und mit dem Ziel gestaltet, Licht einzulassen und Sicht auf die Bucht zu gewähren. Der Rotholz-Hain auf der einen Seite blieb erhalten und ein Weg hindurch angelegt, der zur Haustür und den auf verschiedenen Ebenen liegenden Terrassen führt. Der Besitzer wünschte sich ein minimalistisches Design, Seefahrtselemente für die Terrassen sowie einen offenen Kamin und eine offene Küche im Hauptgeschoss. Wo immer möglich wurden Dachfenster eingebaut, so auch ein großes Viereck in der Mitte von Küche und Wohnbereich. Das große Schlafzimmer liegt am ruhigeren Ende des Hauptgeschosses und führt auf zwei Dachterrassen, verfügt über ein eigenes Bad und einen von oben beleuchteten Schrank.

Completion date: **1996**

Une propriété a été rénovée et repensée pour accueillir la lumière et jouir des vues sur la baie. Le bosquet de séquoias a été préservé pour y tracer une allée menant à l'entrée principale et aux terrasses à plusieurs niveaux. Le propriétaire voulant un design minimaliste a opté pour un décor nautique sur les passerelles extérieures, une cheminée ouverte et un plan ouvert pour le niveau principal. Les claires-voies intégrées autant que possible incluent un quadrilatère au centre de la cuisine et du séjour. La chambre principale se situe du côté calme du niveau principal et accède à deux terrasses, une suite de bain et une penderie à tabatière.

La casa preexistente fue reformada para abrirla a la luz y las vistas de la bahía. Respetando la arboleda de secuoyas de uno de los flancos, se abrió una vereda que conduce hasta la puerta principal y varias cubiertas de múltiples niveles. El propietario deseaba un diseño minimalista y optó por decorar con motivos náuticos las cubiertas exteriores, así como la ancha chimenea y la cocina abierta del piso principal. Se incorporaron tragaluces por doquier, incluyendo un largo cuadrángulo en el centro de la cocina y el salón. El dormitorio principal está situado en la zona más tranquila de la planta baja, y se abre a dos de las cubiertas, un baño y un servicio coronado con una claraboya.

Alvarado Road House

MILLARD T. PRATT AIA WITH SVEN LAVINE
ted@mtparchitects.com

Changes in floor level create different platforms in this contemporary interpretation of the California hillside home. These platforms mark out the various areas in the residence, delineating each space without any need for visible partitions. Materials such as stucco, local stone and terracotta were used along the exterior of the building to evoke the traditional building methods used by the early settlers of the area. Inside, a wide range of materials reflects the client's personality and achievements.

Unterschiedliche Bodenhöhen schaffen verschiedene Plattformen in dieser zeitgenössischen Interpretation des kalifornischen Hauses in Hanglage. Diese Ebenen bestimmen die diversen Wohnbereiche und umreißen jeden Raum, ohne sichtbare Trennelemente nötig zu machen. Materialien wie Stuckgips, Naturstein und Terrakotta wurden außen am Gebäude verwendet, um an traditionelle Baumethoden, wie sie von frühen Siedlern der Gegend angewandt wurden, zu erinnern. Im Inneren unterstreicht eine breite Materialpalette Erfolg und Persönlichkeit des Auftraggebers.

Completion date: **2003**

Les évolutions des niveaux du sol créent plusieurs plates-formes pour cette vision contemporaine de la maison des collines californienne. Ces plates-formes forment des aires de résidence, décrivant chaque espace sans partitions visibles. Le stuc, la pierre native et la terre cuite, utilisés à l'extérieur de l'édifice, évoquent les méthodes de construction d'antan, celles des premiers arrivants. À l'intérieur, une riche palette de matériaux souligne l'identité et les succès du client.

Los cambios de la planta baja crearon diferentes plataformas en una contemporánea interpretación de la típica casa de las colinas de San Francisco. Estas plataformas establecieron áreas habitables diferenciadas, delineando el espacio sin necesidad de ninguna partición visible. En el exterior se utilizaron materiales como el estuco, la piedra autóctona y la terracota para evocar los métodos tradicionales de los primeros habitantes de la zona. En el interior, una rica paleta de materiales recalca la identidad y los logros del cliente.

Second Floor

First Floor

Barnes/Tenazas Residence

STANLEY SAITOWITZ
stanley@saitowitz.com

Situated on the north slope of Bernal Heights on the corner of a cul-de-sac and a public staircase, this residence/ workplace is linked to a pre-existing house by a courtyard. One entrance provides access to the living quarters, the other leads on to the work area. Going upwards, the house begins with a garage, followed by a photography studio, the family sleeping areas and finally, on the top level, the loft with the kitchen, dining and living rooms. A clerestory window lets in light and a round bay window frames the panoramic views. The curve flows through the gridded steel frame of the elevation, adorning the external structure and expressing the logic of the design.

Dieses am Nordhang von Bernal Heights, an der Ecke zwischen einer Sackgasse und einer öffentlichen Trep- pe, gelegene Wohn- und Ateliergebäu- de ist über einen Hof mit einem beste- henden Haus verbunden. Ein Zugang erschließt den Wohn-, der andere den Arbeitsbereich. Von unten nach oben betrachtet beginnt das Haus mit einer Garage, darauf folgen das Fotoatelier, die Schlafräume und schließlich der Loft mit Küche, Ess- und Wohnberei- chen im Obergeschoss. Ein Oberlicht- fenster lässt Licht ein und ein rundes Erkerfenster rahmt den Panoramablick. Die Bogenlinie fließt über den Stahl- gitterrahmen auf die Erhöhung, zum Schmuck der Außenstruktur und als Ausdruck der Logik des Konzepts.

Completion date: **2001**

Sur le flanc nord de Bernal Heights, au coin d'un cul-de-sac et d'un escalier public, cet immeuble de vie/travail est relié par une cour à une demeure existante. Un accès connecte les fonctions de séjour, l'autre la zone de travail. En montant, la maison commence au garage, suivi d'un atelier photo, des chambres à coucher et enfin du loft avec coins cuisine, repas et séjour, au sommet. Une claire-voie apporte la lumière et une baie arrondie encadre des vues panoramiques. la courbe suit le cadre grillagé d'acier vers l'élévation, décorant la structure extérieure et exprimant la logique du plan.

Situada en ladera norte de Bernal Heights, en la esquina de una calle sin salida y una escalera pública, esta residencia y lugar de trabajo se comunica por un patio interior con la casa preexistente. Un acceso lleva a la vivienda; el otro, al área de trabajo. La casa acoge un garaje, sobre éste un estudio de fotografía, los dormitorios, y, finalmente, en el ático, una cocina, un comedor y un salón. Una ventana abuhardillada deja entrar la luz y un ventanal enmarca las vistas panorámicas. La curva fluye a través del enrejado de acero del armazón del alzado, que adorna la estructura exterior y deja entrever la lógica del plan.

First Floor

Second Floor

Third Floor

Fourth Floor

Perkins-Herbert Residence

JENSEN & MACY ARCHITECTS
info@jensen-macy.com

This residence integrates one-off elements into a contemporary living space for a small family. A large central skylight floods the top floor with light, which then passes through a glass floor to the rooms below. In addition to the usual daily needs of a family residence, the clients also wanted a DJ's booth and a dance floor integrated into their home. The Corian-topped kitchen island serves the dual functions of a familiar household feature and a DJ's mixing desk, which is fully integrated into the solid block of the island. This duality extends to the rest of the main living level—by day a brightly lit domestic space, by night a discotheque.

Bei diesem Haus wurden einzigartige Elemente in einen zeitgenössischen Wohnraum für eine kleine Familie integriert. Das Obergeschoss wird über ein großes zentrales Dachfenster von Licht durchflutet, das durch den Glasboden in die darunter liegenden Räume dringt. Zusätzlich zu den üblichen Bedürfnissen eines Familienhaushalts wünschten die Auftraggeber den Einbau einer DJ-Anlage und einer Tanzfläche. Die Kücheninsel mit Corian-Oberfläche erfüllt eine Doppelfunktion als Haushaltselement und DJ-Pult, das vollkommen in den massiven Block der Insel integriert ist. Diese Verwandlung überträgt sich auch auf den Rest dieser zentralen Wohnebene: tagsüber ein hell erleuchteter Hausbereich, wird sie nachts zur Discothek.

Completion date: **2001**

Cette résidence intègre des éléments uniques en un espace de vie moderne pour une petite famille. Une grande claire-voie centrale inonde le haut de lumière et traverse un sol vitré jusqu'aux chambres. Outre les besoins quotidiens d'une demeure familiale, les clients nécessitaient l'intégration d'une platine de DJ et d'une piste de danse. L'îlot de cuisine en Corian sert à la fois de table familiale et de station de DJ, parfaitement intégrée dans le bloc du plan de travail. Cette transformation s'étend au reste du niveau de séjour – de jour un espace domestique gai et de nuit une discothèque.

Esta casa integra elementos únicos en un espacio contemporáneo de vivienda para una familia pequeña. Una gran claraboya central inunda el piso superior de luz, que, por el suelo de cristal, pasa también a las habitaciones de abajo. Además de satisfacer las necesidades diarias de la familia, el cliente quería una cabina de DJ y una pista de baile integradas en su propia casa. La isla de la cocina recubierta de Corian cumple su función doméstica habitual, y al mismo tiempo acoge la cabina del DJ, que está totalmente integrada en el sólido bloque mostrador. Esta transformación se extiende al resto de la planta principal, que de día es un luminoso espacio doméstico y, de noche, una discoteca.

Lower Level

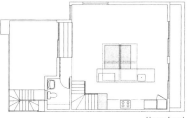

Upper Level

371

Twin Flats

JENSEN & MACY ARCHITECTS
info@jensen-macy.com

This project involved the simultaneous renovation of two nearly identical flats. The interior hallway walls were removed and replaced with full-height translucent sliding glass panels that run along the entire length of each apartment. These panels let light into the core of the apartment and allow rooms to be selectively reconfigured. New service rooms, including the kitchen, guest bathroom, closet and master bathroom, are rendered in a clean modern style with ceramic tiles, dark-stained mahogany and stainless steel. Each of these can be opened or closed off from the main living area by the sliding doors. The lounge, dining room and bedrooms are preserved in their original state.

Bei diesem Projekt wurden zwei nahezu identische Wohnungen gleichzeitig renoviert. Die Wände des Flurs wurden entfernt und durch auf der gesamten Höhe durchsichtige Glasschiebepaneele ersetzt, die sich über die volle Länge der Apartments erstrecken. Diese Paneele lassen Licht ins Herz des Apartments und ermöglichen es, die Räume gezielt umzugestalten. Neue Nutzräume, darunter Küche, Gästebad, WC und großes Badezimmer, sind in klarem modernen Stil mit Fliesen, dunkel gebeiztem Mahagoni und Edelstahl ausgeführt. Jeder einzelne kann durch die Schiebetüren zum Hauptwohnbereich hin geöffnet oder von diesem getrennt werden. Wohn-, Ess- und Schlafzimmer wurden in ihrem ursprünglichen Zustand belassen.

Completion date: **2000**

Ce projet est une rénovation simultanée de deux appartements presque identiques. Les murs du hall intérieur ont été remplacés par des panneaux vitrés translucides coulissants à pleine hauteur, parcourant la longueur de chaque logement. Ces cloisons guident la lumière au cœur de l'appartement et facilitent une reconfiguration sélective. De nouvelles pièces de service – cuisine, bain d'invité, penderie et bain principal – sont modernisées à l'aide de céramiques, d'acajou noirci et d'acier inox. Chacune peut être ouverte ou fermée vis à vis de la zone de séjour par des portes coulissantes. Les autres pièces – séjour, salle à manger, chambres – ont été préservées intactes.

El proyecto llevó a cabo la reforma de dos pisos casi idénticos. Las paredes del pasillo interior se sustituyeron por paneles de cristal traslúcido que van del techo al suelo y se pueden correr todo lo largo de cada apartamento. Estos paneles dejan entrar la luz hasta el corazón de la vivienda, y permiten seleccionar y reconfigurar los espacios discrecionalmente. Las nuevas áreas funcionales, que incluyen la cocina, un baño de invitados, un lavabo y el baño principal, están recubiertas de modernos azulejos de cerámica, caoba oscurecida y acero inoxidable. Cada una de ellas se comunica con el salón principal a través de puertas correderas. Las demás habitaciones –salón, comedor y dormitorios– quedaron en su estado original.

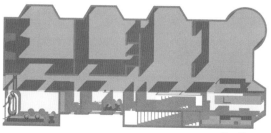

Floor Plan

Choy/Rowley Residence

CARY BERNSTEIN
cbstudio@aol.com

The addition of a third floor provided an opportunity to infuse this 1908 cottage located in the Castro neighborhood with the playful, open and light qualities of contemporary design. A new double-height staircase provides a dramatic entrance, transforming a small cottage into an architectural experience. Open risers, a back-lit cabinet wall and other details emphasize the concept of light and transparency while the solid, steel-clad fireplace creates a perfect balance with the open, sculptural staircase. The exterior deceptively conceals the urban New York-style interiors. Minimalist details stand out against the older, plain shingled building, creating a harmonious dialogue between old and new.

Durch die Aufstockung einer dritten Etage konnte in dieses 1908 erbaute Cottage im Castro-Viertel das Spielerische, Offene und die Leichtigkeit der zeitgenössischen Architektur einfließen. Eine neue, über zwei Stockwerke gehende Treppe macht den Eingang zum Blickfang und das kleine Haus zum architektonischen Erlebnis. Fehlende Setzstufen und eine von hinten beleuchtete Schrankwand unterstreichen neben Anderem Licht und Transparenz. Der massive, stahlverkleidete Kamin stellt das vollkommene Gleichgewicht zur offenen, skulpturalen Treppe her. Das Äußere verschleiert den urbanen New Yorker Stil des Interieurs. Minimalistische Details heben sich vom schindelgedeckten Bau ab und stellen einen harmonischen Dialog zwischen Alt und Neu her.

Completion date: **2002**

L'ajout d'un troisième étage a offert l'occasion d'infuser à ce cottage de 1908 du quartier de Castro la gaîté, l'ouverture et la luminosité d'un design contemporain. Un nouvel escalier à double hauteur crée une entrée spectaculaire, transformant le petit cottage en expérience architecturale. Escalier ajouré, placard rétro-éclairés et autres détails soulignent le concept lumineux et transparent alors que la cheminée d'acier vêtue crée l'équilibre parfait avec l'escalier ouvert et sculptural. L'extérieur reste trompeur sur les intérieurs urbain new-yorkais. Les détails minimalistes rejaillissent de la nature directe de l'ancienne construction, créant un dialogue harmonieux entre l'ancien et le nouveau.

El añadido de un tercer piso dio la oportunidad de dar un aire nuevo a esta cabaña de 1908 del barrio de Castro con un diseño alegre, abierto y luminoso. Una nueva escalera de doble altura crea una entrada espectacular, transformando el estrecho habitáculo en una experiencia arquitectónica. Las contrahuellas abiertas, una pared con iluminación interior y otros detalles enfatizan el concepto de luminosidad y transparencia, mientras que la sólida chimenea revestida de acero logra un perfecto equilibrio con la escalera abierta y escultural. La apariencia exterior oculta el estilo urbano neoyorquino de dentro. Detalles minimalistas contrastan con la sencilla naturaleza de la construcción original de tablillas creando un armonioso diálogo entre moderno y antiguo.

Second Floor

Third Floor

Shah-Conrad Residence

CARY BERNSTEIN
cbstudio@aol.com

Originally a craftsman's house from the early 1900s, this residence was renovated to bring out the best of the original structure by using new and modern materials. The new interior elements are formally expressive and made of different materials from the original shell. Simple geometric forms like the flush cabinet doors, a hanging globe light and the cube-shaped fireplace provide a counterpoint to the articulated paneling, wainscot and molding. The kitchen and dining area open onto a new wooden deck terrace. A variety of modern materials have been used, with stainless steel, cold rolled steel, laminated glass and a laboratory-style countertop standing out as the main elements in the white interior shell.

Dieses ehemalige Handwerkerhaus aus dem frühen 20. Jahrhundert, wurde mit dem Ziel renoviert, durch neue und moderne Materialien das Beste aus dem ursprünglichen Tragwerk herauszuholen. Die neuen Elemente im Inneren sind formal ausdrucksstark und bestehen aus verschiedenen Materialien des Bestands. Schlichte geometrische Formen wie die glatten Schranktüren, eine Kugelhängelampe und ein eckiger Kamin stellen einen Kontrast zu mehrgliedrigen Paneelen, Holzverkleidungen und Zierleisten dar. Der Koch- und Essbereich öffnet sich zu einer neuen hölzernen Dachterrasse. Moderne Elemente wie Edelstahl, kalt gewalztes Stahl, Verbundglas und eine Art Labortischablage treten innerhalb der weiß gehaltenen Umgebung hervor.

Completion date: **1999**

Maison d'artisan du début du siècle, cette résidence a été rénovée pour raviver le meilleur de la structure d'origine à l'aide de matériaux nouveaux et modernes. Les nouveaux éléments intérieurs sont exprimés formellement et matériellement distincts de l'enveloppe originelle. Des formes géométriques simples – portes de placard dépouillées, lustre, cheminée cubique – s'offrent en contrepoint aux panneaux articulés, lambris et moulures. Les coins cuisine et repas s'ouvre sur une nouvelle terrasse en bois. Une palette moderne d'acier inox, de plaquage en acier, de verre feuilleté et un plan de travail de laboratoire sont les éléments principaux des intérieurs immaculés.

Esta casa de un artesano de principios del siglo XX se reformó para resaltar lo mejor de la estructura antigua con la implementación de materiales modernos. Los nuevos elementos interiores se expresan formalmente y los materiales usados resaltan en el armazón original. Las formas geométricas simples de las puertas de los armarios, una lámpara de globo y una chimenea de formas cúbicas son el contrapunto de los paneles articulados, las taraceas y las molduras. La cocina y el comedor se abren a una nueva terraza con cubierta de madera. Una paleta moderna de acero inoxidable, acero, cristal laminado, y la encimera de una mesa de laboratorio destacan como los elementos principales en el interior de la blanca estructura.

First Floor

Second Floor

Other Designpocket titles by teNeues:

Asian Interior Design 3-8238-4527-6

Bathroom Design 3-8238-4523-3

Berlin Apartments 3-8238-5596-4

Cafés & Restaurants 3-8238-5478-X

Cool Hotels 3-8238-5556-5

Country Hotels 3-8238-5574-3

Exhibition Design 3-8238-5548-4

Furniture/Möbel/Meubles/Muebles Design 3-8238-5575-1

Garden Design 3-8238-4524-1

Italian Interior Design 3-8238-5495-X

Kitchen Design 3-8238-4522-5

London Apartments 3-8238-5558-1

Los Angeles Houses 3-8238-5594-8

New York Apartments 3-8238-5557-3

Office Design 3-8238-5578-6

Paris Apartments 3-8238-5571-9

Product Design 3-8238-5597-2

Showrooms 3-8238-5496-8

Spa & Wellness Hotels 3-8238-5595-6

Staircases 3-8238-5572-7

Sydney Houses 3-8238-4525-x

Tokyo Houses 3-8238-5573-5

Each volume:

12.5 x 18.5 cm
400 pages
c. 400 color illustrations